Identity

K[NO]W GOD
K[NO]W YOU

Discovering the real you in Christ Jesus

Zachary N. Taylor

© Zachary N. Taylor, 2018, 1st Edition

ISBN-13: 978-0692174487 (madeforhisimage)

ISBN-10: 0692174486

Cover designed by zachtaylorstudios

Unless otherwise noted, scripture quotations are taken from the Holy Bible, English Standard Version © (ESV©) Copyright © 2001 by Crossway, a publishing ministry of Good News Publishers. Used by permission. All rights reserved.

Scripture quotations marked NIV are taken from the Holy Bible, NEW INTERNATIONAL VERSION ©, NIV © Copyright 1973, 1978, 1984, 2011 by Bilica, Inc. © Used by permission. All rights reserved worldwide.

K[no]w God, K[no]w You

CONTENTS

Introduction 05

Seek first the Kingdom 09

Created for His Image 23

Image Lost 29

Saving that which was lost 41

Dead to sin-Alive to Christ 51

Put on the new 61

Healing: Expression of Love 79

Baptism of the Holy Spirit 91

Spiritual Gifts 99

Conclusion 119

INTRODUCTION

In all your getting, get understanding

First of all, let me say I love you and believe the Lord lead you to read this book for the same reason He put it on my heart to create it. It is imperative we begin to understand who we are because lives are being destroyed each and every day, and it's time we rise up and do something about it! Our lives have so much more value, destiny, and purpose than we understand.

We simply cannot understand who we are and our purpose apart from knowing God!

God says in Hosea 4:6

"My people are destroyed for lack of knowledge."

Isaiah 5:13 says

"Therefore my people go into exile for lack of knowledge."

Proverbs 4:7 (NIV)

"The beginning of wisdom is this: Get wisdom. Though it cost all you have, get understanding."

The truth is, most of us simply don't have a clear understanding of just how good the gospel is and everything we have access to in the finished work of the cross. We are held as captives in our unbelief and lack of understanding. By in large, we simply don't understand who we are in Christ, and we are often indistinguishable from the rest of the world.

I pray that God is starting a fire in your heart at this very moment not to be held captive in a lack of understanding any longer so I proclaim **Luke 4:18 over you...**

"The Spirit of the Lord is upon me, because he has anointed me to proclaim good news to the poor. He has sent me to proclaim liberty to the captives and recovering of sight to the blind, to set at liberty those who are oppressed."

It's time for you to get an understanding of the gospel and let Jesus set you free.

John 8:31-32

"If you abide in my word, you are truly my disciples, and you will know the truth, and the truth <u>will</u> set you free."

Luke 2:10

And the angel said unto them, Fear not: for, behold, I bring you good tidings of great joy, which shall be to all people.

The angels proclaimed on the night Jesus was born that good tidings of great joy were just ushered into the world. If we can get a grasp of the good tidings then there is automatic joy. If you were to understand the good tidings, you would experience the great joy that is available to you every minute of every day no matter what this world throws at you.

Jesus said in John 18:37

"For this purpose I was born and for this purpose I have come into the world–to bear witness to the truth. Everyone who is of the truth listens to my voice,"

So let's set our hearts on understanding the truth about who we really are and embrace our true identity as sons and daughters of the Most High God. It's time to live our lives the way God intended; Knowing Him. In Knowing Him we get to Know ourselves and why we are here.

John 17:3

And this is eternal life, that they know you, the only true God, and Jesus Christ whom you have sent.

John 13:34-35

A new commandment I give to you, that you love one another: just as I have loved you, you also are to love one another. By this all people will know that you are my disciples, if you have love for one another."

1 John 4:7-8

Beloved, let us love one another, for love is from God, and whoever loves has been born of God and knows God. Anyone who does not love does not know God, because God is love.

1 John 4:16

So we have come to know and to believe the love that God has for us. God is love, and whoever abides in love abides in God, and God abides in him.

Matthew 7:21-23

"Not everyone who says to me, 'Lord, Lord,' will enter the kingdom of heaven, but the one who does the will of my Father who is in heaven. On that day many will say to me, 'Lord, Lord, did we not prophesy in your name, and cast out demons in your name, and do many mighty works in your name?' And then will I declare to them, '<u>I never knew you;</u> depart from me, you workers of lawlessness.'

Father I pray you give us a spirit of wisdom and revelation in the knowledge of you and your glory; having the eyes of our hearts enlightened, so that we will have complete hope to all that you have called us to; that we may have full understanding of the riches of your glorious inheritance in the saints, and the immeasurable greatness and power toward us because we believe. May we fully come to understand this power that is according to the working of your great might that worked as you rose Jesus from the dead and seated Him at Your right hand in the heavenly places far above all rule, authority, power, and dominion; far above every name that is named, not only in this age but in the age to come. Thank you for putting all things under the feet of Jesus and making Him head over all things to the church, which is His body, the fullness of Him who fills all in all.

Amen!

(Prayer from Ephesians 1)

Chapter 1

SEEK FIRST THE KINGDOM

....

Let me start out by stating this study is about understanding who you really are; however this understanding has to be filtered through the lens of The Kingdom of God because you can only find your true identity within the Kingdom.

Chances are when you hear the term "Gospel" you have been taught that it means "Good News." In deed that is the case; however what is the "Good News?" I'm sure you have been taught the Good News is the message of Jesus Christ and His teachings. Maybe you were taught the Good News is the message of salvation.

Again, there is truth in these statements; however let's look at what Jesus himself passionately taught throughout the scriptures. Underlining is my emphasis added.

Matthew 9:35

Jesus went throughout all the cities and villages, teaching in their synagogues and proclaiming the <u>gospel of the kingdom</u> and healing every disease and every affliction.

Luke 4:42

And when it was day, he departed and went into a desolate place. And the people sought him and came to him, and would have kept him from leaving them, but he said to them,

"I must preach the <u>good news of the kingdom of God</u> to the other towns as well; for I was sent for this purpose."

Luke 9:1

And he called the twelve together and gave them power and authority over all demons and to cure diseases, and he sent them out to <u>proclaim the kingdom of God</u> and to heal.

Matthew 6:10

<u>Your kingdom come</u>, your will be done, on earth as it is in heaven.

Matthew 4:17

Jesus began to preach, saying, "Repent, <u>for the kingdom of heaven</u> is at hand."

Matthew 4:23

And he went throughout all Galilee, teaching in their synagogues and <u>proclaiming the gospel of the kingdom</u> and healing every disease and every affliction among the people.

Matthew 5:3

"Blessed are the poor in spirit, <u>for theirs is the kingdom of heaven</u>.

Matthew 6:25-33

Therefore I tell you, do not be anxious about your life, what you will eat or what you will drink, nor about your body, what you will put on. Is not life more than food, and the body more than clothing? Look at the birds of the air: they neither sow nor reap nor gather into barns, and yet your heavenly Father feeds them. Are you not of more value than they? And which of you by being anxious can add a single hour to his span of life? And why are you anxious about clothing?

Consider the lilies of the field, how they grow: they neither toil nor spin, yet I tell you, even Solomon in all his glory was not arrayed like one of these. But if God so clothes the grass of the field, which today is alive and tomorrow is thrown into the oven, will he not much more clothe you, O you of little faith? Therefore do not be anxious, saying, 'What shall we eat?' or 'What shall we drink?' or 'What shall we wear?' For the Gentiles seek after all these things, and your heavenly Father knows that you need them all. <u>But seek first the kingdom of God</u> and his righteousness, and all these things will be added to you.

Read Matthew 13 - Matthew 20; The Kingdom of heaven is like, the Kingdom of heaven is like.....

Mark 1:15

The time is fulfilled, and the <u>kingdom of God is at hand</u>; repent and believe in the gospel."

Mark 3:24

If a <u>kingdom</u> is divided against itself, that <u>kingdom</u> cannot stand. And if a house is divided against itself, that house will not be able to stand.

Matthew 5:10

Blessed are those who are persecuted for righteousness' sake, <u>for theirs is the kingdom of heaven.</u>

Matthew 18:1-4

At that time the disciples came to Jesus, saying, "Who is the <u>greatest in the kingdom of heaven?</u>" And calling to him a child, he put him in the midst of them and said, "Truly, I say to you, unless you turn and become like children, <u>you will never enter the kingdom of heaven.</u> Whoever humbles

himself like this child <u>is the greatest in the kingdom of heaven.</u>

Reading through the scriptures we can clearly see Jesus did not teach the "Gospel of Salvation;" however He did passionately teach the **"Gospel of the Kingdom."**

Jesus himself said in **Matthew 12:34**

"out of the abundance of the heart the mouth speaks."

We tend to talk about the things that are most important to us and close to our heart. It's clear as you read through the scriptures, the Kingdom of God was the first priority of Jesus Christ.

As you proceed through this study, you will see that salvation is meant to bring you back into the kingdom. This is where your Father thought of you before he even created the universe. It's your destiny!

Ephesians 1:4

Even as he chose us in him before the foundation of the world, that we should be holy and blameless before him.

Jeremiah 1:5

"Before I formed you in the womb I knew you."

The Kingdom of Heaven is more than a physical place we will go when we die. It is also a place that we can live from and access while we are still on this earth.

You see The Kingdom of Heaven is more than a place; it's also a person. This may sound strange but the Kingdom of Heaven is also our Father, The Father is the Kingdom of Heaven.

The Father is Spirit and does not have a physical form. The Father is eternal. He has no beginning or end. The Father created our spirit in the same image as His Spirit. The Father created us to be one with Him, just as He is one and exists as Father, Son (Jesus), Holy Spirit.

The Son and Holy Spirit are distinct persons that both live within the Father but exist as one God. Through Christ, we have been made sons and daughters of the Father. You could say we are an extension of the Son who also has the Holy Spirit and we also live inside of the Father.

Romans 8:29

For those whom he foreknew he also predestined to be conformed to the image of his Son, in order that he might be the firstborn among many brothers.

John 1:12-13

But to all who did receive him, who believed in his name, he gave the right to become children of God, who were born, not of blood nor of the will of the flesh nor of the will of man, but of God.

John 17:20-21

"I do not ask for these only, but also for those who will believe in me through their word, that they may all be one, just as you, Father, are in me, and I in you, that they also may be in us, so that the world may believe that you have sent me.

It is the Father's will that you step into and live from the Kingdom. It is the Father's will that you step into and live from Him. It is the Father's will that you become one with Him. The Father is the Kingdom.

Luke 12:32

"Fear not, little flock, for it is your Father's good pleasure to give you the kingdom.

It is the Father's will that you and I step into the Kingdom. Jesus is the door to the Kingdom

John 10:9

I am the door. If anyone enters by me, he will be saved and will go in and out and find pasture.

To get into the Kingdom, you have to walk through a narrow door.

Luke 13:24

"Strive to enter through the narrow door. For many, I tell you, will seek to enter and will not be able.

John 14:6-7

Jesus said to him, "I am the way, and the truth, and the life. <u>No one comes to the Father except through me</u>. If you had known me, you would have known my Father also. From now on you do know him and have seen him."

Matthew 7:7-8

"Ask, and it will be given to you; seek, and you will find; knock, and it will be opened to you. For everyone who asks receives, and the one who seeks finds, and to the one who knocks it will be opened.

The Key to the Kingdom is the Blood of Jesus.

Matthew 16:19

I will give you the keys of the kingdom of heaven, and whatever you bind on earth shall be bound in heaven, and whatever you loose on earth shall be loosed in heaven."

Faith is the power to turn the key and walk through the door.

Hebrews 11:6

And without faith it is impossible to please him, for whoever would draw near to God must believe that he exists and that he rewards those who seek him.

Romans 10:9

If you confess with your mouth that Jesus is Lord and believe in your heart that God raised him from the dead, you will be saved.

1 John 5:4

For everyone who has been born of God overcomes the world. And this is the victory that has overcome the world– our faith.

Ephesians 2:8

For by grace you have been saved through faith. And this is not your own doing; it is the gift of God, not a result of works, so that no one may boast.

When you walk through the door (Jesus) you get covered in blood (The Key) You can't pass through the door without being covered in the blood of Christ. When you step through the door, you enter the Kingdom of Heaven. You appear to be covered in blood which in contrast presents you to the Father white as snow.

Psalms 51:7

Purge me with hyssop, and I shall be clean; wash me, and I shall be whiter than snow.

Isaiah 1:18

"Come now, let us reason together, says the Lord: though your sins are like scarlet, they shall be as white as snow; though they are red like crimson, they shall become like wool.

    We must begin to understand some basic principles of how a Kingdom works so that we can start to change the way we think. Let us submit to the Lord and allow Him to reprogram the way we think based on the Kingdom of God.

Romans 12:2

Do not be conformed to this world, but be transformed by the renewal of your mind, that by testing you may discern what is the will of God, what is good and acceptable and perfect.

2 Corinthians 10:5

We destroy arguments and every lofty opinion raised against the knowledge of God, and take every thought captive to obey Christ.

Ephesians 4:17-24

Now this I say and testify in the Lord, that you must no longer walk as the Gentiles do, in the futility of their minds. They are darkened in their understanding, alienated from the life of God because of the ignorance that is in them, due to their hardness of heart. They have become callous and have given themselves up to sensuality, greedy to practice every kind of impurity. But that is not the way you learned Christ!–

assuming that you have heard about him and were taught in him, as the truth is in Jesus, to put off your old self, which belongs to your former manner of life and is corrupt through deceitful desires, and to be renewed in the spirit of your minds, and to put on the new self, created after the likeness of God in true righteousness and holiness.

As we will discover as you continue in this study, our lives were not meant to be ruled by us being king but rather becoming one with the True King; Jesus.

Obviously a kingdom has to be ruled by a King whom sits on the throne. Our Father set His Son on the Throne of His Kingdom. This Throne is also called the Mercy Seat.

In the Old Testament we see this mercy seat (symbolic of the presence of God) as a part of the ark of the covenant within the tabernacle which blood was applied as an atonement for the sins of the people.

Hebrews 9:1-10

Now even the first covenant had regulations for worship and an earthly place of holiness. For a tent was prepared, the first section, in which were the lampstand and the table and the bread of the Presence. It is called the Holy Place. Behind the second curtain was a second section called the Most Holy Place, having the golden altar of incense and the ark of the covenant covered on all sides with gold, in which was a golden urn holding the manna, and Aaron's staff that budded, and the tablets of the covenant. Above it were the cherubim of glory overshadowing the mercy seat. Of these things we cannot now speak in detail.

These preparations having thus been made, the priests go regularly into the first section, performing their ritual duties, but into the second only the high priest goes, and he but once a year, and not without taking blood, which he offers for himself and for the unintentional sins of the people. By this the Holy Spirit indicates that the way into the holy places is not yet opened as long as the first section is still standing (which is symbolic for the present age). According to this arrangement, gifts and sacrifices are offered that cannot perfect the conscience of the worshiper, but deal only with food and drink and various washings, regulations for the body imposed until the time of reformation.

The blood from sacrificed animals that was placed on the mercy seat on what was called the Day of Atonement would act as a propitiation for the sins of the people; however this had to be continuously repeated because this act was only symbolic of what our Father planned to do in order to bring us back into His Kingdom.

Let's keep reading **Hebrews 9:11-28 & Hebrews 10:1-25**

But when Christ appeared as a high priest of the good things that have come, then through the greater and more perfect tent (not made with hands, that is, not of this creation) he entered once for all into the holy places, not by means of the blood of goats and calves but by means of his own blood, thus securing an eternal redemption. For if the blood of goats and bulls, and the sprinkling of defiled persons with the ashes of a heifer, sanctify for the purification of the flesh, how much more will the blood of Christ, who through the eternal Spirit offered himself without blemish to God, purify our conscience from dead works to serve the living God.

Therefore he is the mediator of a new covenant, so that those who are called may receive the promised eternal inheritance, since a death has occurred that redeems them from the transgressions committed under the first covenant. For where a will is involved, the death of the one who made it must be established. For a will takes effect only at death, since it is not in force as long as the one who made it is alive. Therefore not even the first covenant was inaugurated without blood. For when every commandment of the law had been declared by Moses to all the people, he took the blood of calves and goats, with water and scarlet wool and hyssop, and sprinkled both the book itself and all the people, saying, "This is the blood of the covenant that God commanded for you." And in the same way he sprinkled with the blood both the tent and all the vessels used in worship. Indeed, under the law almost everything is purified with blood, and without the shedding of blood there is no forgiveness of sins.

Thus it was necessary for the copies of the heavenly things to be purified with these rites, but the heavenly things themselves with better sacrifices than these. For Christ has entered, not into holy places made with hands, which are copies of the true things, but into heaven itself, now to appear in the presence of God on our behalf. Nor was it to offer himself repeatedly, as the high priest enters the holy places every year with blood not his own, for then he would have had to suffer repeatedly since the foundation of the world. But as it is, he has appeared once for all at the end of the ages to put away sin by the sacrifice of himself. And just as it is appointed for man to die once, and after that comes judgment, so Christ, having been offered once to bear the sins of many, will appear a second time, not to deal with sin but to save those who are eagerly waiting for him.

For since the law has but a shadow of the good things to come instead of the true form of these realities, it can never, by the same sacrifices that are continually offered every year, make perfect those who draw near. Otherwise, would they not have ceased to be offered, since the worshipers, having once been cleansed, would no longer have any consciousness of sins? But in these sacrifices there is a reminder of sins every year. For it is impossible for the blood of bulls and goats to take away sins.

Consequently, when Christ came into the world, he said, "Sacrifices and offerings you have not desired, but a body have you prepared for me; in burnt offerings and sin offerings you have taken no pleasure. Then I said, 'Behold, I have come to do your will, O God, as it is written of me in the scroll of the book.'"

When he said above, "You have neither desired nor taken pleasure in sacrifices and offerings and burnt offerings and sin offerings" (these are offered according to the law), then he added, "Behold, I have come to do your will." He does away with the first in order to establish the second. And by that will we have been sanctified through the offering of the body of Jesus Christ once for all.

And every priest stands daily at his service, offering repeatedly the same sacrifices, which can never take away sins. But when Christ had offered for all time a single sacrifice for sins, he sat down at the right hand of God, waiting from that time until his enemies should be made a footstool for his feet. For by a single offering he has perfected for all time those who are being sanctified.

And the Holy Spirit also bears witness to us; for after saying, "This is the covenant that I will make with them after those days, declares the Lord: I will put my laws on their hearts, and write them on their minds," then he adds, "I will remember their sins and their lawless deeds no more." Where there is forgiveness of these, there is no longer any offering for sin.

After Jesus rose from the dead we see Jesus telling Mary not to cling to Him.

John 20:17-18

Jesus said to her, "Do not cling to me, for I have not yet ascended to the Father; but go to my brothers and say to them, I am ascending to my Father and your Father, to my God and your God.'" Mary Magdalene went and announced to the disciples, "I have seen the Lord"—and that he had said these things to her.

This was Jesus telling her I'm about to ascend to my Father, who is also your Father, and place my blood on the Mercy Seat once for all, officially establishing My Kingdom, and I'm inviting you all in.

Hebrews 9:12

He entered once for all into the holy places, not by means of the blood of goats and calves but by means of his own blood, thus securing an eternal redemption.

Hebrews 1:3

He is the radiance of the glory of God and the exact imprint of his nature, and he upholds the universe by the word of his power. After making purification for sins, he sat down at the right hand of the Majesty on high.

Religion has been trying to tell us that The Gospel is about us getting to heaven one day in the future. This mindset robs us of the reality that we become partakers of The Kingdom now!

Jesus taught us how to pray and think.

Matthew 6:10

"Your kingdom come, your will be done, on earth as it is in heaven.

Matthew 6:33

But seek first the kingdom of God and his righteousness, and all these things will be added to you.

    Let's continue unfolding The Gospel and allow God to teach us who we really are and why we are here; always keeping in mind that our true identity lies within the Kingdom of God.

Chapter 2

CREATED FOR HIS IMAGE

Genesis 1:26;27;28;3:25

Then God said, "Let us make man in our image, after our likeness......So God created man in his own image, in the image of God he created him; male and female he created them.....And God blessed them. And God said to them, "Be fruitful and multiply and fill the earth and subdue it and have dominion..... And the man and his wife were both naked and were not ashamed.

Here we have an account of God's eternal purpose for mankind or you could say the eternal will of God. You never have to wonder "I wish I knew God's will for my life." The truth is God sent Jesus to uncover the mystery of His will hidden for ages past. The fullness of God and His will has been revealed to us!

"Let us make man in our image, after our likeness"

Here we see the first aspect of understanding God's will. You were created for the image of God. If you could use one word to describe the image of God, what would it be?

1 John 4:8

God is love

John 3:16

For God so loved the world, that he gave his only Son, that whoever believes in him should not perish but have eternal life.

The image of God is love.

"Be fruitful and multiply"

What did He mean by being fruitful? In the Hebrew Language, this word means to bring forth, to grow, to increase.

To bring forth what? To grow in what? To increase what? His image!

"Be fruitful and multiply."

Multiply what? Is He really talking about multiplying ourselves. Is He simply talking about sexual reproduction? No! He is talking about multiplying His image.

It was God's will from the beginning that man <u>bring forth</u> His image. That we would <u>grow into</u> His image. That we would <u>increase in</u> His image and then <u>multiply that image</u> and fill the earth with His glory. It's God's will that every man and woman on earth would bear His image of love. TO BECOME LOVE! This is who God created us to be.

He said "have dominion over the fish of the sea and over the birds of the heavens and over every living thing that moves on the earth."

Part of bearing the image of God is that man would have authority over creation. This authority was because man was one with God. God gave man His authority over creation. This authority was both physical and spiritual. We will talk more about this authority later.

"the man and his wife were both naked and were not ashamed."

What does this mean?

Lets look at Isaiah 61:10

"I will greatly rejoice in the Lord; my soul shall exult in my God, for he has clothed me with the garments of salvation; he has covered me with the robe of righteousness."

This is a picture of the future work of the cross. Adam and Eve were originally created in the righteousness of Christ. They were made in the image of Jesus Christ and wore His robes of righteousness. They were perfect and no shame was upon them. They were in perfect co-union with God. They did not know they were naked because they were covered in garments of salvation and wore robes of righteousness.

John 1:1-4

In the beginning was the Word, and the Word was with God, and the Word was God. He was in the beginning with God. All things were made through him, and without him was not anything made that was made. In him was life, and the life was the light of men.

Colossians 1:15-16

He (Jesus) is the image of the invisible God, the firstborn of all creation. For by him all things were created, in heaven and on earth, visible and invisible, whether thrones or dominions or rulers or authorities—all things were created through him and for him.

We were created by Christ, through Christ and for Christ. The very life of Jesus Christ was put inside Adam and Eve. **"In him was life, and the life was the light of men."**

Genesis 2:7

"then the Lord God formed the man of dust from the ground and breathed into his nostrils the breath of life, and the man became a living creature."

Man was just a form until the life of God was deposited inside of him.

THE PINNACLE OF ALL GOD'S CREATION WAS MAN– BUT NOT JUST MAN BUT GOD IN MAN!

Colossians 1:16-27

"the mystery hidden for ages and generations but now revealed to his saints. To them God chose to make known how great among the Gentiles are the riches of the glory of this mystery, which is Christ in you, the hope of glory."

It always was and is God's will that man carry the image of God in a holy relationship with Him. Again, what is the image of God. LOVE! Who is the image of the invisible God?

Colossians 1:15

(JESUS) He is the image of the invisible God.

Adam and Eve were created by Christ, through Christ, and for Christ. God wants to be so close and intimate with His creation that He wants to live inside of man. You can't get any closer than that. Do you get how intimate that is? God wants a place to dwell and that place is inside of you and me.

So there they are, Adam and Eve in perfect relationship with the Father, the Son, and the Holy Spirit. The very life of Jesus Christ breathed inside of them. Perfect co-union with God. They are one with Him. They are Holy because He is holy. There lives did not belong to them. They belonged to Christ. They were made for Him. They were created to be a vessel that Jesus would pour His love into every second of every day. They became a visible image of the invisible God. Their destiny was to grow in the love of Christ, to bring forth the love of Christ as His creation matured, to increase the image of God throughout the earth, to fill the earth with His glory, and rule with His righteousness! They were created to receive love and return love because they were created by love, through love, and for love.

Everything was perfect and the way God intended it. They were right smack dab in the middle of God's good, pleasing, and perfect will! Again, what was God's will? To look like Him! To be one with Him! To bring forth His image! To grow in His love! To increase the image of God! Fully and freely giving everything they fully and freely received. They were born of God, not by the desire of flesh. It was all God's choosing.

Genesis 1:31

"And God saw everything that He had made, and behold, it was very good"

And that's the way it stayed right?

Chapter 3

IMAGE LOST

Last chapter we began to dive into God's will for creating mankind. We discovered God's will is that we look like Him! To be one with Him! To bring forth His image! To grow in His love! To increase the image of God! TO BECOME LOVE!

So Adam and Eve were in perfect co-union with God; however this isn't the way it stayed. You may know the story; God put Adam and Eve in the Garden of Eden, gave them dominion over everything, established them in perfect union with Himself, and gave them one clear instruction geared toward fostering relationship.

Genesis 1:15

"The Lord God took the man and put him in the garden of Eden to work it and keep it. And the Lord God commanded the man, saying, "You may surely eat of every tree of the garden, but of the tree of the knowledge of good and evil you shall not eat, for in the day that you eat of it you shall surely die."

In this moment, God introduced Adam and Eve to free will and faith. Adam and Eve were given the opportunity to fully believe and trust God. To establish faith in the goodness of God and His Word. So we are introduced to another aspect of understanding God's will; Faith.

What is faith?

Hebrews 11:1-2;6

Now faith is the assurance of things hoped for, the conviction of things not seen. For by it the people of old received their commendation.......And without faith it is impossible to please him, for whoever would draw near to God must believe that he exists and that he rewards those who seek him.

In the beginning, God said the only thing you have to do to please me is have faith. Notice God did not make Adam and Eve do anything to earn His love and acceptance. They were already loved and accepted. God said the only thing you have to "do" to please me is have faith. Have faith in my Word! Have faith in my truth! Have faith in my provision for you! Have faith in my love for you!

So God has purposed, or willed, that Adam and Eve bear His image and place their faith in Him. So here is a question for you? When was sin first introduced into existence? When Adam and Eve ate the fruit from the tree of the knowledge of good and evil right?

Wrong! Sin had already been introduced into existence some time before this. When? In the heavenly realms.

Remember **Genesis 1:1**

"In the beginning, God created the heavens and the earth."

At some unknown amount of "time", God created the heavens, or the spiritual realm, before He created the physical realm. How all this played out is irrelevant and beyond our understanding. The simple truth we are highlighting is that there is a spiritual realm and a physical realm. During this time we are introduced to one of God's most beautiful created angels. His name is Lucifer.

Ezekiel 28:12-19

"You were the signet of perfection, full of wisdom and perfect in beauty. You were in Eden, the garden of God; every precious stone was your covering, sardius, topaz, and diamond, beryl, onyx, and jasper, sapphire, emerald, and carbuncle; and crafted in gold were your settings and your engravings. On the day that you were created they were prepared. You were an anointed guardian cherub. I placed you; you were on the holy mountain of God; in the midst of the stones of fire you walked. You were blameless in your ways from the day you were created, till unrighteousness was found in you. In the abundance of your trade you were filled with violence in your midst, and you sinned; so I cast you as a profane thing from the mountain of God, and I destroyed you, O guardian cherub, from the midst of the stones of fire. Your heart was proud because of your beauty; you corrupted

your wisdom for the sake of your splendor. I cast you to the ground; I exposed you before kings, to feast their eyes on you. By the multitude of your iniquities, in the unrighteousness of your trade you profaned your sanctuaries; so I brought fire out from your midst; it consumed you, and I turned you to ashes on the earth in the sight of all who saw you. All who know you among the peoples are appalled at you; you have come to a dreadful end and shall be no more forever.

Lucifer was perfect in all his ways and he was a specially anointed angel. I think it is safe to say that he was God's most special angel, and the most beautiful angel with the most splendor. However; we see here that Lucifer became so impressed with himself; with his own beauty, intelligence, power, and position, that he began to desire for himself the honor and glory that belonged to God alone. The sin that corrupted Lucifer was self-generated pride and lead to rebellion against the Creator.

Isaiah 14:12-17 God tells us Lucifer said in his heart...

I will ascend to heaven; above the stars of God. I will set my throne on high. I will sit on the mount of assembly in the far reaches of the north. I will ascend above the heights of the clouds. I will make myself like the Most High.

Lucifer wanted to become God and take His place as god over his own life! He was created to guard Adam & Eve. He was entrusted with God's most precious belongings. He didn't want to serve man, He wanted to be served and worshipped by man. The sin of self pride entered into existence and said "I" am god.

The "god of self" entered into existence. Ultimately this sin is called selfish ambition.

Philippians 2:3

Do nothing from selfish ambition or conceit, but in humility count others more significant than yourselves.

James 3:14-16

But if you have bitter jealousy and selfish ambition in your hearts, do not boast and be false to the truth. This is not the wisdom that comes down from above, but is earthly, unspiritual, demonic. For where jealousy and selfish ambition exist, there will be disorder and every vile practice.

For this Lucifer was judged by God and cast down from heaven and became an enemy of God. From this point on you know what became the strategy of the enemy. STEAL-KILL-DESTROY.

John 10:10

The thief comes only to steal and kill and destroy

Satan with his attempt to steal the image of God and have it all for himself now wants to steal the image of God in man. He wants the authority that God gave man. We wants to destroy the faith that man has in God. He wants man to die and be forever ensnared along with him. And in the process of all of this, he wants to deceive man into believing its all God's fault! STEAL-KILL-DESTROY; STEAL-KILL-DESTROY; BLAME GOD; BLAME GOD!

1 Peter 5:8

Be sober-minded; be watchful. Your adversary the devil prowls around like a roaring lion, seeking someone to devour.

How does satan implement his strategy? By introducing doubt about the goodness of God, the love of God, the truth of God, and their true identity in Him. It all started with posing a question. "Did God really say?" This question was designed to attack their faith in a good God and everything they were in Him. To destroy the image of God in them and turn them into gods unto themselves just like satan. You could say that Satan's will is to make men in his image and reproduce after his own kind.

Genesis 3:1-7

Now the serpent was more crafty than any other beast of the field that the Lord God had made. He said to the woman, "Did God actually say, 'You shall not eat of any tree in the garden'?" And the woman said to the serpent, "We may eat of the fruit of the trees in the garden, but God said, 'You shall not eat of the fruit of the tree that is in the midst of the garden, neither shall you touch it, lest you die.'" But the serpent said to the woman, "You will not surely die. For God knows that when you eat of it your eyes will be opened, and you will be like God, knowing good and evil." So when the woman saw that the tree was good for food, and that it was a delight to the eyes, and that the tree was to be desired to make one wise, she took of its fruit and ate, and she also gave some to her husband who was with her, and he ate. Then the eyes of both were opened, and they knew that they

were naked. And they sewed fig leaves together and made themselves loincloths.

So did satan's strategy work? It sure did! But here's a question. Did they die? Did they physically drop dead and die right in that moment when they ate the fruit? So what died? This was a spiritual death.

God in man died, or the image of God died in man, and man once again became just a form of what God created man to be. Their eyes were opened to the fact they were naked.

Remember, before they did not know they were naked because they were clothed in garments of salvation; robes of righteousness. Now they are naked and feel ashamed and here we see the first attempts to cover our own sin. To deceive ourselves into thinking we can do something about our sin problem. **they sewed fig leaves together and made themselves loincloths.** The image of God in man died!

Faith died! *"For God knows that when you eat of it your eyes will be opened, and you will be like God, knowing good and evil."*

Adam and Eve lost their faith in a Good God by believing at least two lies here.

1. That God was holding something back from them. That He hadn't given them everything.

So when the woman saw that the tree was good for food, and that it was a delight to the eyes, and that the tree was to be desired to make one wise, she took of its fruit and

ate, and she also gave some to her husband who was with her, and he ate. In this moment we see self desire begin. Adam and Eve's self desire began. The desire for God died and the god of self awakened. The truth is, they had everything! God had given all of Himself to them.

2. That they were not like God! **But the serpent said to the woman, "You will not surely die. For God knows that when you eat of it your eyes will be opened, and you will be like God."** They were deceived into believing they could become something they already were! They were created in the image of God! They were like God!

So there they stand; Faith stolen from them, The image of God killed, Everything God created man for; destroyed. STEAL-KILL-DESTROY; STEAL-KILL-DESTROY The only thing left to make satan's strategy complete is for God to take the blame for everything.

Genesis 3:8-13

And they heard the sound of the Lord God walking in the garden in the cool of the day, and the man and his wife hid themselves from the presence of the Lord God among the trees of the garden. But the Lord God called to the man and said to him, "Where are you?" And he said, "I heard the sound of you in the garden, and I was afraid, because I was naked, and I hid myself." He said, "Who told you that you were naked? Have you eaten of the tree of which I commanded you not to eat?" The man said, "<u>The woman whom you gave</u> to be with me, <u>she gave me</u> fruit of the tree, and I ate." Then the Lord God said to the woman, "What is

this that you have done?" The woman said, "The serpent deceived me, and I ate.

Notice Adam fresh in sin says hey God don't blame me, It was the WOMAN YOU gave me! Eve says it was the SERPENTS fault. And now the full effects of sin have begun. The god of self is fully alive. Self preservation, self centeredness at the cost of someone else. Blame shifting and back biting have begun.

So here is the question. What was the original sin? Why did we inherit sin from Adam and not Eve? Because Adam was the first person to sin, not Eve!

Satan's strategy to make man in his image succeeded. Adam fell victim to the exact same sin that Lucifer did; selfish ambition! Let's look at this again.

Genesis 3:6-7

So when the woman saw that the tree was good for food, and that it was a delight to the eyes, and that the tree was to be desired to make one wise, she took of its fruit and ate, and she also gave some to her husband who was with her, and he ate. Then the eyes of both were opened, and they knew that they were naked. And they sewed fig leaves together and made themselves loincloths.

Notice the scripture says "she gave some to her husband who was with her." So picture this. Adam was standing there the whole time when Satan was filling Eve's head with lies. What was going through Adam's mind during all of this? He was starting to believe the lies just like Eve was and beginning to be filled with the same doubts. I believe Adam wanted to eat the fruit;

however I believe he certainly remembered God saying if you eat this fruit you shall surly die! So Adam was willing to allow his wife to eat the fruit so he could see what happened to her. Would she die? Could what Satan was saying be true? Eve ate the fruit and did not drop dead so Adam was willing to take the fruit and eat also.

What Adam should have done is immediately respond to Satan and his attempts to subvert the will of God and put a stop to this; however selfish ambition was ushered into mankind and Satan was able to reproduce after his own kind in that moment. Adam totally sold his wife out and blamed her for his fall!

Does any of this look like love? No! Because the image of God has died. **The day you eat of the tree is the day that you surely die!** Also note the image of God died the moment Adam decided in his heart to let Eve eat the fruit, not when they actually ate the fruit. Can you recall Jesus teaching on this concept? "You say, but I say…"

You know what else happened that day? The authority and dominion over the earth God gave to Adam and Eve was handed over to Satan. They gave it away. And now Satan has authority and dominion over this world. He has become the god of this world.

Romans 11:29

For the gifts and the calling of God are irrevocable.

Matthew 4:8-9

Again, the devil took him to a very high mountain and showed him all the kingdoms of the world and their glory. And he said to him, "All these I will give you, if you will fall down and worship me.

Ephesians 6:11-12

Put on the whole armor of God, that you may be able to stand against the schemes of the devil. For we do not wrestle against flesh and blood, but against the rulers, against the authorities, against the cosmic powers over this present darkness, against the spiritual forces of evil in the heavenly places.

2 Corinthians 4:4

In their case the god of this world has blinded the minds of the unbelievers, to keep them from seeing the light of the gospel of the glory of Christ, who is the image of God.

Ephesians 2:2

And you were dead in the trespasses and sins in which you once walked, following the course of this world, following the prince of the power of the air, the spirit that is now at work in the sons of disobedience.

John 14:30-31

I will no longer talk much with you, for the ruler of this world is coming. He has no claim on me, but I do as the Father has

commanded me, so that the world may know that I love the Father.

What horrible news! Satan seems to have won. Darkness has overcome light. Sin has infiltrated the world and subdued it. The image of God in man has been destroyed. Faith has been lost. Sickness and death ushered into the earth. The earth itself cursed. Authority handed over to the enemy. Mankind has been cut off from eternal life. Relationship and intimacy with our Father; gone! Everything and was created to be and become has been lost. And to top it all off, everyone blames God! Sounds like we could really use some good news right about now.

Praise be to our God and Father of our Lord Jesus Christ who came to seek and save that which was lost!!

Chapter 4

SAVING THAT WHICH WAS LOST

We left off with darkness overcoming light; however here is question for you. Can darkness really overcome light? Have you ever asked someone to turn up the darkness? Of course not because we all know light always overcomes darkness. The Good News is that Jesus came to restore everything that was lost in the fall of man.

Luke 19:10

For the Son of man came to seek and to save that which was lost.

What was lost? The image of God! God in man! Our identity as sons and daughters of God! Our intimacy and relationship with the Father! Authority and Dominion! Our original created value! Our Destiny! Our Purpose! It's all about love, identity, and relationship; and it was all lost in the garden.

John 3:16

"For God so loved the world, that he gave his only Son, that whoever believes in him should not perish but have eternal life.

What is eternal life?

John 17:1-3

When Jesus had spoken these words, he lifted up his eyes to heaven, and said, "Father, the hour has come; glorify your Son that the Son may glorify you, since you have given him authority over all flesh, to give eternal life to all whom you have given him. And this is eternal life, that they know you the only true God, and Jesus Christ whom you have sent.

Jesus shed His blood to bring us back into relationship with the Father! Jesus took us back to the beginning of all things and restored our original created value. We have been restored back to love! It's what we were created for!

John 14:6

Jesus said… "I am the way, and the truth, and the life. No one comes to the Father except through me.

Notice it does not say; "No one comes to heaven except through me." Christianity is about coming back to the Father and bearing His image of love! The finished work of the cross is not when you pray a prayer to get into heaven, but when your nature is changed back to love. Remember…we were created to bear the image of God. We are to BECOME love!

Genesis 1:26;27

Then God said, "Let us make man in our image, after our likeness…..So God created man in his own image, in the image of God he created him.

1 John 4:8

Anyone who does not love does not know God, because God is love.

1 John 4:16

So we have come to know and to believe the love that God has for us. God is love, and whoever abides in love abides in God, and God abides in him.

We were created to become one with God! This is how we bear His image of love.

John 17

When Jesus had spoken these words, he lifted up his eyes to heaven, and said, "Father, the hour has come; glorify your Son that the Son may glorify you, since you have given him authority over all flesh, to give eternal life to all whom you have given him. And this is eternal life, that they know you the only true God, and Jesus Christ whom you have sent. I glorified you on earth, having accomplished the work that you gave me to do. And now, Father, glorify me in your own presence with the glory that I had with you before the world existed.

"I have manifested your name to the people whom you gave me out of the world. Yours they were, and you gave them to me, and they have kept your word. Now they know that everything that you have given me is from you. For I have given them the words that you gave me, and they have received them and have come to know in truth that I came from you; and they have believed that you sent me. I am praying for them. I am not praying for the world but for those whom you have given me, for they are yours. All mine are yours, and yours are mine, and I am glorified in them. And I am no longer in the world, but they are in the world, and I am coming to you. Holy Father, keep them in your name, which you have given me, that they may be one, even as we are one. While I was with them, I kept them in your name, which you have given me. I have guarded them, and not one of

them has been lost except the son of destruction, that the Scripture might be fulfilled. But now I am coming to you, and these things I speak in the world, that they may have my joy fulfilled in themselves. I have given them your word, and the world has hated them because they are not of the world, just as I am not of the world. I do not ask that you take them out of the world, but that you keep them from the evil one. They are not of the world, just as I am not of the world. Sanctify them in the truth; your word is truth. As you sent me into the world, so I have sent them into the world. And for their sake I consecrate myself, that they also may be sanctified in truth.

"I do not ask for these only, but also for those who will believe in me through their word, that they may all be one, just as you, Father, are in me, and I in you, that they also may be in us, so that the world may believe that you have sent me. The glory that you have given me I have given to them, that they may be one even as we are one, I in them and you in me, that they may become perfectly one, so that the world may know that you sent me and loved them even as you loved me. Father, I desire that they also, whom you have given me, may be with me where I am, to see my glory that you have given me because you loved me before the foundation of the world. O righteous Father, even though the world does not know you, I know you, and these know that you have sent me. I made known to them your name, and I will continue to make it known, that the love with which you have loved me may be in them, and I in them.

    We should not make a practice of reducing the Bible into a book with a bunch of promises in order for our day to be better. Christianity is not a self-centered and self-focused way of life. We are called to die to ourselves and live free. If we make it all about us, then we will get consumed with life and how everything is going and begin to wonder where God is in the midst. God lives in you and wants to manifest Himself through you. It's not about everything going your way but rather revealing Him. It's not about us. It's about Him.

Romans 8:29-30

For those whom he foreknew he also predestined to be conformed to the image of his Son, in order that he might be the firstborn among many brothers. And those whom he predestined he also called, and those whom he called he also justified, and those whom he justified he also glorified.

Colossians 1:15-23

He is the image of the invisible God, the firstborn of all creation. For by him all things were created, in heaven and on earth, visible and invisible, whether thrones or dominions or rulers or authorities—all things were created through him and for him. And he is before all things, and in him all things hold together. And he is the head of the body, the church. He is the beginning, the firstborn from the dead, that in everything he might be preeminent. For in him all the fullness of God was pleased to dwell, and through him to reconcile to himself all things, whether on earth or in heaven, making peace by the blood of his cross. And you, who once were alienated and hostile in mind, doing evil deeds, he has now reconciled in his body of flesh by his death, in order to present you holy and blameless and above reproach before him, if indeed you continue in the faith, stable and steadfast, not shifting from the hope of the gospel that you heard, which has been proclaimed in all creation under heaven, and of which I, Paul, became a minister.

    Jesus said...

Matthew 16:24-25

"If anyone would come after me, let him deny himself and take up his cross and follow me. For whoever would save his life will lose it, but whoever loses his life for my sake will find it.

We don't go to church to receive something from God; to get our needs met; but rather we come together to look more like Him. To be transformed into His image and become more equipped to go.

2 Peter 1:3-11

His divine power has granted to us all things that pertain to life and godliness, through the knowledge of him who called us to his own glory and excellence, by which he has granted to us his precious and very great promises, so that through them you may become partakers of the divine nature, having escaped from the corruption that is in the world because of sinful desire. For this very reason, make every effort to supplement your faith with virtue, and virtue with knowledge, and knowledge with self- control, and self-control with steadfastness, and steadfastness with godliness, and godliness with brotherly affection, and brotherly affection with love. For if these qualities are yours and are increasing, they keep you from being ineffective or unfruitful in the knowledge of our Lord Jesus Christ. For whoever lacks these qualities is so nearsighted that he is blind, having forgotten that he was cleansed from his former sins. Therefore, brothers, be all the more diligent to confirm your calling and election, for if you practice these qualities you will never fall. For in this way there will be richly provided for you an entrance into the eternal kingdom of our Lord and Savior Jesus Christ.

He has given us His precious and very great promises, SO THAT through them we can partake of His divine nature! To be like Him! To manifest Him! To become love! Everything you need for peace, joy, happiness ect.. comes from the Lord, not people or things.

Luke 2:10

And the angel said to them, "Fear not, for behold, I bring you good news of great joy that will be for all the people.

Romans 15:13

May the God of hope fill you with all joy and peace in believing, so that by the power of the Holy Spirit you may abound in hope.

John 16:22

So also you have sorrow now, but I will see you again, and your hearts will rejoice, and no one will take your joy from you.

The barometer of your life should never be people or things. You need to look through the eyes of God. To look at who God sees you to be and then you will see others for who God created them to be.

Luke 22:37-40

And he said to him, "You shall love the Lord your God with all your heart and with all your soul and with all your mind. This is the great and first commandment. And a second is like it: You shall love your neighbor as yourself. On these two commandments depend all the Law and the Prophets.

If you can't get a good grip on who you are and your value in the eyes of God, then you will never see the value in others. In reality we all wear the same price tag! We are all worth the blood of Christ.

Romans 5:8

but God shows his love for us in that while we were still sinners, Christ died for us.

John 3:16

"For God so loved the world, that he gave his only Son, that whoever believes in him should not perish but have eternal life.

1 John 4:10-21

In this the love of God was made manifest among us, that God sent his only Son into the world, so that we might live through him. In this is love, not that we have loved God but that he loved us and sent his Son to be the propitiation for our sins. Beloved, if God so loved us, we also ought to love one another. No one has ever seen God; if we love one another, God abides in us and his love is perfected in us. By this we know that we abide in him and he in us, because he has given us of his Spirit. And we have seen and testify that the Father has sent his Son to be the Savior of the world. Whoever confesses that Jesus is the Son of God, God abides in him, and he in God. So we have come to know and to believe the love that God has for us. God is love, and whoever abides in love abides in God, and God abides in him. By this is love perfected with us, so that we may have confidence for the day of judgment, because as he is so also are we in this world. There is no fear in love, but perfect love casts out fear. For fear has to do with punishment, and whoever fears has not been perfected in love. We love because he first loved us. If anyone says, "I love God," and hates his brother, he is a liar; for he who does not love his brother whom he has seen cannot love God whom he has not

seen. And this commandment we have from him: whoever loves God must also love his brother.

You love Him, because He first loved you! You love others, because He first loved you! Jesus came and restored us back to the beginning. We have been redeemed. Our original created value, destiny, and purpose has been restored.

Everything that was lost in the garden has been given back to us through the blood of Christ! The identity of sinner has been broken and replaced with the identity of sonship! So from this point on we simply need to learn how to live as sons and daughters.

Chapter 5

DEAD TO SIN-ALIVE TO CHRIST

Truth: God does not see us as sinners, He sees us as sons and daughters! The Gospel is not something that exposes your sin and makes you realize you're nothing but a sinner. The Gospel reveals your value and that your life was worth the blood of Christ. Your life means something to God. The Gospel doesn't expose your sin, it removes your sin so you can get along with simply being a son or daughter. Sin is no longer our problem! Righteousness is! We have been made clean!

1 John 1:9

If we confess our sins, he is faithful and just to forgive us our sins and to cleanse us from all unrighteousness.

1 John 3:5

You know that he appeared in order to take away sins, and in him there is no sin.

Romans 6:2

How can we who died to sin still live in it?

Romans 6:11

So you also must consider yourselves dead to sin and alive to God in Christ Jesus.

2 Corinthians 5:18-21

All this is from God, who through Christ reconciled us to himself and gave us the ministry of reconciliation; that is, in Christ God was reconciling the world to himself, not counting their trespasses against them, and entrusting to us the message of reconciliation. Therefore, we are ambassadors for Christ, God making his appeal through us. We implore you on behalf of Christ, be reconciled to God. For our sake he made him to be sin who knew no sin, so that in him we might become the righteousness of God.

John 1:12-13

But to all who did receive him, who believed in his name, he gave the right to become children of God, who were born, not of blood nor of the will of the flesh nor of the will of man, but of God.

Galatians 3:26

For in Christ Jesus you are all sons of God, through faith.

Romans 8:16

The Spirit himself bears witness with our spirit that we are children of God.

Hear is another truth. We don't have to wake up each day and try to be a christian. You are a son/daughter, You are accepted and not rejected. You do not have to live your day feeling condemned any longer. Righteousness covers you and grace empowers you! You can now wake up every single day as a son/daughter! You are in a love relationship! He is your Father and you only have to learn how to be a son/daughter! The identity of sinner has been removed and replaced with the identity of sonship so reckon yourself dead to sin! You are already accepted, received and loved! It's not about failing, it's about being His! He has purified your heart and is in the process of perfecting you in Christ Jesus. Satan will always try to condemn your pure heart. The things that bother you about your life is simply the result of a new and pure heart. Satan will continue to try and condemn your pure heart. Don't listen to him.

Philippians 1:6

And I am sure of this, that he who began a good work in you will bring it to completion at the day of Jesus Christ.

Revelation 12:10-11 *(Underlined my emphasis)*

And I heard a loud voice in heaven, saying, "Now the salvation and the power and the kingdom of our God and the authority of his Christ have come, for the accuser of our brothers has been thrown down, who accuses them day and night before our God. And they have conquered him <u>by the blood of the Lamb</u> and <u>by the word of their testimony</u>, <u>for they loved not their lives even unto death.</u>

Here are two things, you should not think about much or give much weight to. Sin and Satan. Instead, replace these two thoughts with Jesus Christ and Sonship. We should not make much of the things that don't need to made much of. We should make much of the love of God, the finished work of the cross, Mercy, Grace, Freedom, and the power of God in you!

Colossians 3:2-3

Set your minds on things that are above, not on things that are on earth. For you have died, and your life is hidden with Christ in God. When Christ who is your life appears, then you also will appear with him in glory.

Proverbs 4:25

Let your eyes look directly forward, and your gaze be straight before you.

2 Corinthians 10:5-7

We destroy arguments and every lofty opinion raised against the knowledge of God, and take every thought captive to obey Christ, being ready to punish every disobedience, when your obedience is complete. Look at what is before your eyes. If anyone is confident that he is Christ's, let him remind himself that just as he is Christ's, so also are we.

1 Peter 1:13-16

Therefore, preparing your minds for action, and being sober-minded, set your hope fully on the grace that will be brought to you at the revelation of Jesus Christ. As obedient children, do not be conformed to the passions of your former

ignorance, but as he who called you is holy, you also be holy in all your conduct, since it is written, "You shall be holy, for I am holy.

Philippians 4:8

Finally, brothers, whatever is true, whatever is honorable, whatever is just, whatever is pure, whatever is lovely, whatever is commendable, if there is any excellence, if there is anything worthy of praise, think about these things.

Romans 12:2

Do not be conformed to this world, but be transformed by the renewal of your mind, that by testing you may discern what is the will of God, what is good and acceptable and perfect.

Remember, the enemy is cursed and was last seen crawling on his belly. In Revelations we see him as a seven headed monster. How did he get that way? Man gave him power by fearing him and giving him honor, creating this monster. All the while Jesus is Lord!

Satan knows there is absolutely nothing he can do to stop the wisdom and power of God. He was there when the tomb was rolled away and watched Jesus raise from the dead defeating death! But; Satan definitely believes he can stop man and God in man by confusing them of their true identity. He thinks he can stop you! He wants to keep you self-centered, sin conscious, divided, and lead you into arguments and debating with your brothers and sisters in Christ. His power lies in his ability to blind you of the truth. His power lies in what you fail to see.

2 Corinthians 4:4-6

In their case the god of this world has blinded the minds of the unbelievers, to keep them from seeing the light of the gospel of the glory of Christ, who is the image of God. For what we proclaim is not ourselves, but Jesus Christ as Lord, with ourselves as your servants for Jesus 'sake. For God, who said, "Let light shine out of darkness," has shone in our hearts to give the light of the knowledge of the glory of God in the face of Jesus Christ.

Matthew 16:23

But he turned and said to Peter, "Get behind me, Satan! You are a hindrance to me. For you are not setting your mind on the things of God, but on the things of man."

God sent His Son and redeemed your created value! You were taken back to the beginning! LOVE! Jesus said follow me as the first born of many to come!

Matthew 4:19

And he said to them, "Follow me, and I will make you fishers of men."

Matthew 16:24

Then Jesus told his disciples, "If anyone would come after me, let him deny himself and take up his cross and follow me.

Colossians 1:15

He is the image of the invisible God, the firstborn of all creation.

Guilt, Condemnation, and Shame have to end! They are tools of the devil! You did not pray a prayer to go to heaven. You got heaven back inside of you! It's time to put off the old and put on the new! You were not created for yourself but for the glory of God! You were created to bear the image of God. If you are not becoming love then you have missed the whole purpose of your new birth! The bible says the goal of all our instruction is love.

1 Timothy 1:5

But the goal of our instruction is love from a pure heart and a good conscience and a sincere faith.

Ephesians 4:22-24

Put off your old self, which belongs to your former manner of life and is corrupt through deceitful desires, and to be renewed in the spirit of your minds, and to put on the new self, created after the likeness of God in true righteousness and holiness.

Colossians 3:9-10

Do not lie to one another, seeing that you have put off the old self with its practices and have put on the new self, which is being renewed in knowledge after the image of its creator.

Romans 6:6-8

We know that our old self was crucified with him in order that the body of sin might be brought to nothing, so that we would no longer be enslaved to sin. For one who has died has been set free from sin.

Isaiah 43:1-7

But now thus says the Lord, he who created you, O Jacob, he who formed you, O Israel: "Fear not, for I have redeemed you; I have called you by name, you are mine. When you pass through the waters, I will be with you; and through the rivers, they shall not overwhelm you; when you walk through fire you shall not be burned, and the flame shall not consume you. For I am the Lord your God, the Holy One of Israel, your Savior. I give Egypt as your ransom, Cush and Seba in exchange for you. Because you are precious in my eyes, and honored, and I love you, I give men in return for you, peoples in exchange for your life. Fear not, for I am with you; I will bring your offspring from the east, and from the west I will gather you. I will say to the north, Give up, and to the south, Do not withhold; bring my sons from afar and my daughters from the end of the earth, everyone who is called by my name, whom I created for my glory, whom I formed and made.

Psalm 86:12

I give thanks to you, O Lord my God, with my whole heart, and I will glorify your name forever.

John 13:34-35

A new commandment I give to you, that you love one another: just as I have loved you, you also are to love one another. By this all people will know that you are my disciples, if you have love for one another."

1 John 4:-7-10

Beloved, let us love one another, for love is from God, and whoever loves has been born of God and knows God. Anyone who does not love does not know God, because God is love.

1 Corinthians 13:1-13

And I will show you a still more excellent way. If I speak in the tongues of men and of angels, but have not love, I am a noisy gong or a clanging cymbal. And if I have prophetic powers, and understand all mysteries and all knowledge, and if I have all faith, so as to remove mountains, but have not love, I am nothing. If I give away all I have, and if I deliver up my body to be burned, but have not love, I gain nothing. Love is patient and kind; love does not envy or boast; it is not arrogant or rude. It does not insist on its own way; it is not irritable or resentful; it does not rejoice at wrongdoing, but rejoices with the truth. Love bears all things, believes all things, hopes all things, endures all things. Love never ends. As for prophecies, they will pass away; as for tongues, they will cease; as for knowledge, it will pass away. For we know in part and we prophesy in part, but when the perfect comes, the partial will pass away. When I was a child, I spoke like a child, I thought like a child, I reasoned like a child. When I became a man, I gave up childish ways. For now we see in a mirror dimly, but then face to face. Now I know in part; then I shall know fully, even as I have been fully known. So now faith, hope, and love abide, these three; but the greatest of these is love.

You are the bride of Christ and you look so good to Him! Faith works through love. We are not trying to have faith, We are pursuing knowing God! When you know God who is love, faith is the spontaneous result of knowing God. You don't live for God, but through God. That means your identity becomes one with Him.

1 John 4:9-11

In this the love of God was made manifest among us, that God sent his only Son into the world, so that we might live through him. In this is love, not that we have loved God but that he loved us and sent his Son to be the propitiation for our sins. Beloved, if God so loved us, we also ought to love one another.

Your identity becomes what Jesus accomplished! Jesus did not die on the cross so you could serve Him from afar; He did it for union and spiritual intimacy. This new life in Christ is about transformation. Accepting the grace of God apart from transformation is a perversion of God's grace. It's about putting off the old and putting on the new and becoming who God created you to be.

Chapter 6

PUT ON THE NEW

. . . .

The term repentance simply means to turn away from living for yourself. To walk away from self-centeredness and committing to renew how you think. To put on the new self and wear your new identity.

Matthew 4:17

From that time Jesus began to preach, saying, "Repent, for the kingdom of heaven is at hand."

Ephesians 4:22-24

Put off your old self, which belongs to your former manner of life and is corrupt through deceitful desires, and to be renewed in the spirit of your minds, and to put on the new self, created after the likeness of God in true righteousness and holiness.

2 Corinthians 7:10

For godly grief produces a repentance that leads to salvation without regret, whereas worldly grief produces death.

Matthew 26:28

For this is my blood of the covenant, which is poured out for many for the forgiveness of sins.

Do not make the mistake of praying a prayer to get into heaven as your motivation of accepting Jesus. You must understand you are becoming one with God; and putting off an old nature and putting on a new nature. It's time to throw away selfishness and be clothed in love. Ask the Holy Spirit to manifest the heart of God to you and begin to thank Him that His heart is yours. Ask Him to give you the eyes to start seeing what He sees. Pursue a relationship, not just biblical knowledge so you can try to apply biblical principles in order for your life or your day to be better.

Pursue face to face intimacy! Remember, you died before you were born again, so you can really live. You died in the likeness of Jesus' death and He died to sin once for all so sin can't be the issue anymore. You have been resurrected from the dead with Christ and have been made righteous, so rise to the newness of life!

John 3:3-8

Jesus answered him, "Truly, truly, I say to you, unless one is born again he cannot see the kingdom of God." Nicodemus said to him, "How can a man be born when he is old? Can he enter a second time into his mother's womb and be born?" Jesus answered, "Truly, truly, I say to you, unless one is born of water and the Spirit, he cannot enter the kingdom of God. That which is born of the flesh is flesh, and that which is born

of the Spirit is spirit. Do not marvel that I said to you, 'You must be born again.' The wind blows where it wishes, and you hear its sound, but you do not know where it comes from or where it goes. So it is with everyone who is born of the Spirit.

Matthew 16:24-28

Then Jesus told his disciples, "If anyone would come after me, let him deny himself and take up his cross and follow me. For whoever would save his life will lose it, but whoever loses his life for my sake will find it. For what will it profit a man if he gains the whole world and forfeits his soul? Or what shall a man give in return for his soul? For the Son of Man is going to come with his angels in the glory of his Father, and then he will repay each person according to what he has done. Truly, I say to you, there are some standing here who will not taste death until they see the Son of Man coming in his kingdom.

Romans 6:1-14

What shall we say then? Are we to continue in sin that grace may abound? By no means! How can we who died to sin still live in it? Do you not know that all of us who have been baptized into Christ Jesus were baptized into his death? We were buried therefore with him by baptism into death, in order that, just as Christ was raised from the dead by the glory of the Father, we too might walk in newness of life. For if we have been united with him in a death like his, we shall certainly be united with him in a resurrection like his. We know that our old self was crucified with him in order that the body of sin might be brought to nothing, so that we would no longer be enslaved to sin. For one who has died has been set free from sin. Now if we have died with Christ, we believe that we will also live with him. We know that Christ, being raised from the dead, will never die again; death no longer has dominion over him. For the death he died he died to sin, once for all, but the life he lives he lives to God. So you also must consider yourselves dead to sin and alive to God in Christ Jesus. Let not sin therefore reign in your mortal body, to make you obey its passions. Do not present your members to sin as instruments for unrighteousness, but present yourselves to God as those who have been brought from death to life, and your members to God as instruments for righteousness. For sin will have no dominion over you, since you are not under law but under grace.

1 Peter 3:18

For Christ also suffered once for sins, the righteous for the unrighteous, that he might bring us to God, being put to death in the flesh but made alive in the spirit.

2 Corinthians 5:17

Therefore, if anyone is in Christ, he is a new creation. The old has passed away; behold, the new has come.

Jesus died to bring you back to your original created value. The Gospel was never meant to expose your failures and make you see you are nothing but a sinner, but rather highlight how much you are worth to God. You are the Pearl of Great Price!

Matthew 13:45-46

"Again, the kingdom of heaven is like a merchant in search of fine pearls, who, on finding one pearl of great value, went and sold all that he had and bought it.

You see, The Gospel isn't about you! It's about being transformed into His image.

2 Corinthians 3:18

And we all, with unveiled face, beholding the glory of the Lord, are being transformed into the same image from one degree of glory to another. For this comes from the Lord who is the Spirit.

Satan believes you have accepted Christ strictly for yourself. He believes you are only in this for what you can get from God and how you can be blessed by God. Satan doesn't believe you love God more than your own life, but he does believe you need God for your own life and he accuses you night and day before The Father. The way we overcome these accusations is by the blood of the lamb, the word of our testimony and we love not our own life unto death. Satan's accusation to the Father is always yes you do; you love your own life! It's all about you!

Revelation 12:9-11

And the great dragon was thrown down, that ancient serpent, who is called the devil and Satan, the deceiver of the whole world– he was thrown down to the earth, and his angels were thrown down with him. And I heard a loud voice in heaven, saying, "Now the salvation and the power and the kingdom of our God and the authority of his Christ have come, for the accuser of our brothers has been thrown down, who accuses them day and night before our God. And they have conquered him by the blood of the Lamb and by the word of their testimony, for they loved not their lives even unto death.

2 Corinthians 1:8-11

For we do not want you to be unaware, brothers, of the affliction we experienced in Asia. For we were so utterly burdened beyond our strength that we despaired of life itself. Indeed, we felt that we had received the sentence of death. But that was to make us rely not on ourselves but on God who raises the dead. He delivered us from such a deadly peril, and he will deliver us. On him we have set our hope that he will deliver us again. You also must help us by prayer, so that many will give thanks on our behalf for the blessing granted us through the prayers of many.

2 Corinthians 4:8-12

We are afflicted in every way, but not crushed; perplexed, but not driven to despair; persecuted, but not forsaken; struck down, but not destroyed; always carrying in the body the death of Jesus, so that the life of Jesus may also be manifested in our bodies. For we who live are always being given over to death for Jesus 'sake, so that the life of Jesus also may be manifested in our mortal flesh. So death is at work in us, but life in you.

Most of the adversity you will face in your life is designed to expose the motives of your heart. What usually happens when a christian gets squeezed by the troubles of this life, everything but Jesus typically comes spilling out. That should not be our response. Satan has learned that when a christian gets squeezed, all kinds of things come out; ultimately revealing our motives are unsettled, unsure, and therefore makes us pretty good targets for more adversity to come our way. We make ourselves vulnerable by responding to trials this way. Satan is locating what makes you tick. He doesn't believe you love God more than your own life, but for your own life.

How would you respond to trials if you were free from yourself! *"If any man comes after me, he must deny himself."* Cry out in the words of John the Baptist.. "Free me from me Lord! Increase so I can decrease!" With a shift in mindset, when you face trials and the harder you are squeezed, all the more Jesus can come out. Satan should begin thinking twice about poking you because it's just going to draw you closer to Jesus and more love will be spread all around you. Satan's pokes on you will only cause his kingdom to be destroyed not advanced!

You were created for God's image and because you were born into Adam, you inherently became self-centered. You have to deny yourself to be born again and be restored back to love. You are to be freed from yourself. And now it's all about Him in you!

The evidence of being free from you is that you are free from people! If you're free from people, then all you can do is love them! People or things can never be the basis of how your day is going. People shouldn't ever have the power to ruin your day. You are called to love people so how can someones misconduct affect you if you're in Christ and He's in you, and he loves people? It then becomes a *"forgive them Father for they know not what they do."*

You see from the time you were born, you desperately needed someone to love and appreciate you. We have accepted this as a normal pattern of life, but that's the way we became through sin! You were created to love but because of sin you were cut off from the source of true love so now you need love. So now you have been trying your whole life to find love and acceptance everywhere but in Him. We think it's normal to let people hurt us, disappoint us, and break our trust, but it's all the fall of man! It's not normal!

I hear a lot of talk about setting up boundaries with people, but you only need to set up boundaries if you are vulnerable. Why even put an expectation on someone and give them an opportunity offend you when Jesus is Lord, and we are called to love! Why would we set someone up to fail us or disappoint us and begin to think their value is less than it really is by putting expectations on them? If we need people to treat us the right way in this life to have joy, we are not going to have joy! We should not give that much power to anyone. We are called to love people so we should never let sin against us produce sin in us!

We have all been through trials in our life. Some much more than others! The temptation is to make your story lord of your life instead of making His Story Lord! Don't be deceived into thinking it's all about you, your rights, how you were offended, or how you were wronged by someone!

2 Corinthians 5:14-21

For the love of Christ controls us, because we have concluded this: that one has died for all, therefore all have died; and he died for all, that those who live might no longer live for themselves but for him who for their sake died and was raised. From now on, therefore, we regard no one according to the flesh. Even though we once regarded Christ according to the flesh, we regard him thus no longer. Therefore, if anyone is in Christ, he is a new creation. The old has passed away; behold, the new has come. All this is from God, who through Christ reconciled us to himself and gave us the ministry of reconciliation; that is, in Christ God was reconciling the world to himself, not counting their trespasses against them, and entrusting to us the message of reconciliation. Therefore, we are ambassadors for Christ, God making his appeal through us. We implore you on behalf of Christ, be reconciled to God. For our sake he made him to be sin who knew no sin, so that in him we might become the righteousness of God.

In Christ all things are new! You have new purpose, new value, new destiny, and a new identity! Remember, the finished work of Christ is not when you pray a prayer to go to heaven, but when your nature is changed back to love! Redemption is being brought back to your original created value!

It's time to see yourself as you were created to be then you will be able to see how to love your neighbor as yourself! Begin to see people for their value and ask God to show you the potential in every man and woman; how to look past the behavior they are manifesting into the very essence of who they were created to be! By doing this, you can treat people according to their original created value, look at their potential and determine their worth to treat them with love and honor.

Colossians 3:1-17

If then you have been raised with Christ, seek the things that are above, where Christ is, seated at the right hand of God. Set your minds on things that are above, not on things that are on earth. For you have died, and your life is hidden with Christ in God. When Christ who is your life appears, then you also will appear with him in glory. Put to death therefore what is earthly in you: sexual immorality, impurity, passion, evil desire, and covetousness, which is idolatry. On account of these the wrath of God is coming. In these you too once walked, when you were living in them. But now you must put them all away: anger, wrath, malice, slander, and obscene talk from your mouth. Do not lie to one another, seeing that you have put off the old self with its practices and have put on the new self, which is being renewed in knowledge after the image of its creator. Here there is not Greek and Jew, circumcised and uncircumcised, barbarian, Scythian, slave, free; but Christ is all, and in all. Put on then, as God's chosen ones, holy and beloved, compassionate hearts, kindness, humility, meekness, and patience, bearing with one another and, if one has a complaint against another, forgiving each other; as the Lord has forgiven you, so you also must forgive. And above all these put on love, which binds everything together in perfect harmony. And let the peace of Christ rule in your hearts, to which indeed you were called in one body. And be thankful. Let the word of Christ dwell in you richly, teaching and admonishing one another in all wisdom, singing psalms and hymns and spiritual songs, with thankfulness in your hearts to God. And whatever you do, in word or deed, do everything in the name of the Lord Jesus, giving thanks to God the Father through him.

Set your heart at becoming love, and when you come together with your brothers and sisters in Christ, encourage each other in love but don't ever get caught in the trap of comparing yourself with anyone. Don't ever think what you are doing to love people is more or less important than what someone else is doing. Whatever you are doing in love is touching the person and growing you. The power of love is amazing! You can't fail when you are in love!

When you are out sharing The Gospel, don't beat people up and draw out the need for what Jesus can do for them. The goal is not to get them to pray a prayer and draw them across the line to Jesus so he can meet their needs. You step across the line, love them, and see how mercy and love triumph over judgment. People will cross the line over to Jesus because He is so lovely and amazing, not for what He can do for them. We having to stop preaching Jesus is here to meet all your needs and deliver you from this life. Don't use people's needs to power play them to accept Jesus. Simply love people, let love cover over a multitude of sin, and let the goodness of God cause people to repent. It's time to begin loving people with no strings attached!

1 Peter 4:8

Above all, keep loving one another earnestly, since love covers a multitude of sins.

2 Timothy 2:24-26

And the Lord's servant must not be quarrelsome but kind to everyone, able to teach, patiently enduring evil, correcting his opponents with gentleness. God may perhaps grant them repentance leading to a knowledge of the truth, and they may come to their senses and escape from the snare of the devil, after being captured by him to do his will.

Romans 2:4

Or do you presume on the riches of his kindness and forbearance and patience, not knowing that God's kindness is meant to lead you to repentance?

2 Corinthians 7:10

For godly grief produces a repentance that leads to salvation without regret, whereas worldly grief produces death.

2 Corinthians 5:16-21

From now on, therefore, we regard no one according to the flesh. Even though we once regarded Christ according to the flesh, we regard him thus no longer. Therefore, if anyone is in Christ, he is a new creation. The old has passed away; behold, the new has come. All this is from God, who through Christ

reconciled us to himself and gave us the ministry of reconciliation; that is, in Christ God was reconciling the world to himself, not counting their trespasses against them, and entrusting to us the message of reconciliation. Therefore, we are ambassadors for Christ, God making his appeal through us. We implore you on behalf of Christ, be reconciled to God. For our sake he made him to be sin who knew no sin, so that in him we might become the righteousness of God.

The Lord has given us the ministry of reconciliation! He is calling us to reconcile people back to God so we must make it our mission to love people unconditionally with the heart of God.

We devalue the finished work of the cross when we fail to see people or ourselves any other way than God sees us. False humility is destroying our identity! The truth is the person you were before Christ is dead! You have been born again into an entirely new identity. You are not a sinner saved by grace! You are a son or a daughter saved by grace! All things are new! The old you is gone! You are not a better version of the old you, you are a completely new person. It's not a fresh start, it's a new start!

Understanding the fullness of your new identity in Christ is the first step in becoming a world changer who advances the Kingdom of God. If you don't know who you are neither will anyone else. God's will is that you live a supernaturally transformed life of influence on this earth. It's not about praying a prayer to go to heaven. It's getting heaven back inside of you! Jesus restored your original created value! You were created to bear His image of love, power, and authority.

He has given us everything to live the lives He has destined us for! You are supernatural, amazing and miraculous! You are a living manifestation of God to this world! You and I were created to be living expressions of contradiction to natural limitations! So it's time to stop seeing yourself as anything less than what God says you are. Let's take a look at another example in Scripture that proclaims your identity.

Matthew 7:17-18

So, every healthy tree bears good fruit, but the diseased tree bears bad fruit. A healthy tree cannot bear bad fruit, nor can a diseased tree bear good fruit.

Matthew 12:33

"Either make the tree good and its fruit good, or make the tree bad and its fruit bad, for the tree is known by its fruit.

Be honest! When you read these scriptures on good fruit it often discourages you doesn't it? You think to yourself "man, my fruit isn't looking good so I must not be good." Sometimes you may struggle with and wonder if you are even saved at all.

I want to encourage you to stop focusing on the fruit! These scriptures are not focusing on the fruit, but rather on the tree! When you make the tree good, then it will bear good fruit! So what you need to realize is that you ARE a good tree! This is your identity in Christ Jesus! You stand holy, righteous and blameless in His sight! His love for you is full throttle all the time. You are so precious and perfect to Him. You are His masterpiece! You are worth His blood so throw out any doubt!!

You think your ability to sin identifies you as a sinner, but that simply isn't true! "Have you ever said or heard the phrase "I'm just a sinner saved by grace brother?" That is a lie from hell and not the truth about who you are anymore! That's a bad tree. When you see yourself as a bad tree, you will bear bad fruit. Your identity in Christ is not "sinner", but holy, righteous and redeemed. You are a new creation, restored back to your original created value! "Recon yourself dead to sin!" Your are a saint! You ARE a good tree.

It's time to start seeing yourself for who you really are and stop listening to your enemies voice telling you you are a bad tree! Jesus said His sheep listen to His voice and that He knows them, so they follow Him. Jesus made you a good tree by the free gift of His marvelous grace showered upon you! Put off that old thinking and be transformed by renewing your mind. Those whom He as justified (just-if-I'd never sinned) live by this kind of faith. It's time to see yourself for who you really are in Christ! It's time to receive and believe that YOU ARE A GOOD TREE!!!

Hopefully by this point you have a better understanding of the Gospel and are beginning to understand the tremendous value you have to God. It should no longer be a mystery why God sent His Son to die for you. He had to die for you. He is Love and you and I are His greatest passion.

We have begun to unpack the eternal will of God and have learned that ultimately we were **created for His image** as sons and daughters. We were created by love, through love and for love.

At this point if you have not given your Life to Christ and been water baptized here is the next step for you.

Prayer:

Lord Jesus, I give you my life. I choose to die so I can truly live.

Thank you for shedding your blood and dying for me so I can live for you.

I ask you to fill me with your Holy Spirit, who is the guarantee of my sonship.

Father, thank you for bringing me back to you and restoring everything you created me for.

I receive my sonship and the Lordship of Jesus Christ.

Thank you for making me new today.

I repent from old ways of thinking and I will allow you to renew my mind within my new identity found in Christ Jesus.

Amen!

Baptism: The wedding ring of your covenant love relationship with God.

"Father, I receive this water baptism as the wedding ring of my covenant love relationship with you, bought by the blood of Jesus."

Step into the waters of baptism; symbolizing the denial of yourself, the willingness to lay your life and rights down, as you stand there in the water (symbolic of the grave).

Then **in the likeness of His death**, you pick up your cross and die with Christ; the old you being crucified with Christ as you are lowered into the water. You are dying and the old you is being put into the grave. **("Therefore reckon yourself dead to sin.")**

As you are raised out of the water, you proclaim you have been resurrected with Christ! You have been born again. All things are new! Your true life is now found in Christ Jesus.

Your life no longer belongs to you because it doesn't exist. You died! Your old life is still in the grave so don't pick it back up. Now you are free to truly live! **This is the mystery hidden for ages. Christ in you the hope of glory. It's no longer I who live but Christ who lives in me.**

Congratulations! All things are new! You are a son/daughter!

You have been Made for His Image!

Chapter 7

HEALING: EXPRESSION OF LOVE

It is settled! We are established in our identity in Christ Jesus! We are sons and daughters of God! Deeply loved by our Father! We are the Body of Christ! The earthly manifestation of God's love! We are the Bride of Christ! Intimately bonded as one to our Lord!

In view of our identity, we were created to become Love. Our lives are no longer our own but rather lived as an expression of God. We have died and come alive to Christ Jesus so we can truly live! We have been born again to a new and living way inside the Kingdom of God! We get to spend the rest of our lives simply loving people and exercising the authority and power we have been given in Christ Jesus! **You were Made for His Image!**

One of the biggest manifestations of love we see from the life of Jesus is healing the sick. Sickness and death are not the will of God! We have to settle this question in our minds! Is it the will of God to heal? The answer is YES and AMEN!

2 Corinthians 1:20-22

For all the promises of God find their Yes in him. That is why it is through him that we utter our Amen to God for his glory. And it is God who establishes us with you in Christ, and has anointed us, and who has also put his seal on us and given us his Spirit in our hearts as a guarantee.

We must get our theology from the life of Christ, because Jesus is perfect theology. Jesus is the perfect will of God. We cannot afford to lower the truth of God's Word to our level of experience or our inexperience. We must come to this realization and never create doctrine that we cannot find in the person of Jesus Christ. He is the will of God!

We must put our faith in God's Word not our experiences. It is imperative we stop living a sensual lifestyle. We are called to live by faith not feelings. We live by faith not our experiences.

Romans 1:16-17

For I am not ashamed of the gospel, for it is the power of God for salvation to everyone who believes, to the Jew first and also to the Greek. For in it the righteousness of God is revealed from faith for faith, as it is written, "The righteous shall live by faith."

Romans 5:1-2

Therefore, since we have been justified by faith, we have peace with God through our Lord Jesus Christ. Through him we have also obtained access by faith into this grace in which we stand, and we rejoice in hope of the glory of God.

Hebrews 11:6

And without faith it is impossible to please him, for whoever would draw near to God must believe that he exists and that he rewards those who seek him.

Hebrews 12:1-2

Therefore, since we are surrounded by so great a cloud of witnesses, let us also lay aside every weight, and sin which clings so closely, and let us run with endurance the race that is set before us, looking to Jesus, the founder and perfecter of our faith, who for the joy that was set before him endured the cross, despising the shame, and is seated at the right hand of the throne of God.

James 5:14-15

Is anyone among you sick? Let him call for the elders of the church, and let them pray over him, anointing him with oil in the name of the Lord. <u>And the prayer of faith</u> will save the one who is sick, and the Lord will raise him up. And if he has committed sins, he will be forgiven.

In Luke Chapter 7 we see a story of faith that Jesus himself marveled at.

Luke 7:1-10

After he had finished all his sayings in the hearing of the people, he entered Capernaum. Now a centurion had a servant who was sick and at the point of death, who was highly valued by him. When the centurion heard about Jesus, he sent to him elders of the Jews, asking him to come and heal his servant. And when they came to Jesus, they pleaded with him earnestly, saying, "He is worthy to have you do this for him, for he loves our nation, and he is the one who built us our synagogue." And Jesus went with them. When he was not far from the house, the centurion sent friends, saying to him, "Lord, do not trouble yourself, for I am not worthy to have you come under my roof. Therefore I did not presume to come to you. But say the word, and let my servant be healed. For I too am a man set under authority, with soldiers under me: and I say to one, 'Go,' and he goes; and to another, 'Come,' and he comes; and to my servant, 'Do this,' and he does it." When Jesus heard these things, he marveled at him, and turning to the crowd that followed him, said, "I tell you, not even in Israel have I found such faith." And when those

who had been sent returned to the house, they found the servant well. (Authority, Faith, Healing)

We must live by faith not experiences or feelings. Jesus is the author and perfecter of our faith. God is our Great Potter! Not Life's experiences. Do not let life mold you into it's image. You were predestined before the foundation of the world to be conformed to the image of Jesus Christ our Lord!

Romans 8:29-30

For those whom he foreknew he also predestined to be conformed to the image of his Son, in order that he might be the firstborn among many brothers. And those whom he predestined he also called, and those whom he called he also justified, and those whom he justified he also glorified.

Mark 11:22-25

And Jesus answered them, "Have faith in God. Truly, I say to you, whoever says to this mountain, Be taken up and thrown into the sea,' and does not doubt in his heart, but believes that what he says will come to pass, it will be done for him. Therefore I tell you, whatever you ask in prayer, believe that you have received it, and it will be yours. And whenever you stand praying, forgive, if you have anything against anyone, so that your Father also who is in heaven may forgive you your trespasses."

James 1:5-8

If any of you lacks wisdom, let him ask God, who gives generously to all without reproach, and it will be given him. But let him ask in faith, with no doubting, for the one who doubts is like a wave of the sea that is driven and tossed by the wind. For that person must not suppose that he will receive anything from the Lord; he is a double-minded man, unstable in all his ways.

However; all the faith in the world is useless unless it's done through love. For we were created by love, through love, and for love. Faith works and flows through love. If we have faith that can move mountains but not have love it counts as nothing. Love is everything. We were created to become love.

1 Corinthians 13:1-3

If I speak in the tongues of men and of angels, but have not love, I am a noisy gong or a clanging cymbal. And if I have prophetic powers, and understand all mysteries and all knowledge, and if I have all faith, so as to remove mountains, but have not love, I am nothing. If I give away all I have, and if I deliver up my body to be burned, but have not love, I gain nothing.

How can we look at the life of Christ and not determine healing is the will of God? Jesus taught it, modeled it, sent His disciples out to do it, and gave authority to all who will just believe.

Matthew 6:9-10

Pray then like this: "Our Father in heaven, hallowed be your name. Your kingdom come, your will be done, on earth as it is in heaven.

Is there sickness in heaven? Pain? Torment? How about things like perfect health, peace, joy, contentment? Remember before we flow in the power of God we must be rooted in the heart of God! Love must be our motivation. God's will on earth as it is in heaven has to begin with the heart of God before the power of God! We can be healed because Jesus paid the price for our healing.

1 Peter 2:24-25

He himself bore our sins in his body on the tree, that we might die to sin and live to righteousness. By his wounds you have been healed. For you were straying like sheep, but have now returned to the Shepherd and Overseer of your souls.

Hebrews 13:8

Jesus Christ is the same yesterday and today and forever.

Matthew 4:23

And he went throughout all Galilee, teaching in their synagogues and proclaiming the gospel of the kingdom and healing every disease and every affliction among the people.

Luke 9:10-11

On their return the apostles told him all that they had done. And he took them and withdrew apart to a town called Bethsaida. When the crowds learned it, they followed him, and he welcomed them and spoke to them of the kingdom of God and cured those who had need of healing.

"The Apostles told him all that they had done." What did the Apostles do? What Jesus instructed them to.

Matthew 10:1

And he called to him his twelve disciples and gave them authority over unclean spirits, to cast them out, and to heal every disease and every affliction.

Matthew 10:5-8

These twelve Jesus sent out, instructing them, "Go nowhere among the Gentiles and enter no town of the Samaritans, but go rather to the lost sheep of the house of Israel. And proclaim as you go, saying, The kingdom of heaven is at hand.' Heal the sick, raise the dead, cleanse lepers, cast out demons. You received without paying; give without pay.*

This was not just for the Apostles!!!

Luke 10:1-2 Jesus Sends Out the Seventy-Two

After this the Lord appointed seventy-two others and sent them on ahead of him, two by two, into every town and place where he himself was about to go. And he said to them, "The harvest is plentiful, but the laborers are few. Therefore pray earnestly to the Lord of the harvest to send out laborers into his harvest.

Matthew 9:35-37

And Jesus went throughout all the cities and villages, teaching in their synagogues and proclaiming the gospel of the kingdom and healing every disease and every affliction. When he saw the crowds, he had compassion for them, because they were harassed and helpless, like sheep without a shepherd. Then he said to his disciples, "The harvest is plentiful, but the laborers are few; therefore pray earnestly to the Lord of the harvest to send out laborers into his harvest."

Mark 16:16-18

Whoever believes and is baptized will be saved, but whoever does not believe will be condemned. And these signs will accompany those who believe: in my name they will cast out demons; they will speak in new tongues; they will pick up serpents with their hands; and if they drink any deadly poison, it will not hurt them; they will lay their hands on the sick, and they will recover."

So who does Jesus say will lay their hands on the sick and they will recover? Whoever believes! The evidence of what you believe is a life lived. If you believe, you will lay your hands on the sick and the sick will recover. Get out there and start putting your hands on people. Remember, we live by faith not experiences and anything done in love has great power! Just keep believing in the truth! These signs shall follow those who believe! Continue to grow in your faith and keep asking God for more revelation.

Even if you don't see anything happen, continue to increase in your faith and keep pressing forward. It is always God's will to heal! Don't let your mind talk you out of everything Jesus shed his blood for you to possess.

Matthew 17:14-20

And when they came to the crowd, a man came up to him and, kneeling before him, said, "Lord, have mercy on my son, for he is an epileptic and he suffers terribly. For often he falls into the fire, and often into the water. And I brought him to your disciples, and they could not heal him." And Jesus answered, "O faithless and twisted generation, how long am I to be with you? How long am I to bear with you? Bring him here to me." And Jesus rebuked the demon, and it came out of him, and the boy was healed instantly. Then the disciples came to Jesus privately and said, "Why could we not cast it out?" He said to them, "Because of your little faith. For truly, I say to you, if you have faith like a grain of mustard seed, you will say to this mountain, 'Move from here to there,' and it will move, and nothing will be impossible for you."

Acts 4:23-31

When they were released, they went to their friends and reported what the chief priests and the elders had said to them. And when they heard it, they lifted their voices together to God and said, "Sovereign Lord, who made the heaven and the earth and the sea and everything in them, who through the mouth of our father David, your servant, said by the Holy Spirit,

"'Why did the Gentiles rage, and the peoples plot in vain? The kings of the earth set themselves, and the rulers were gathered together, against the Lord and against his Anointed'—for truly in this city there were gathered together against your holy servant Jesus, whom you anointed, both Herod and Pontius Pilate, along with the Gentiles and the peoples of Israel, to do whatever your hand and your plan had predestined to take place. And now, Lord, look upon their threats and grant to your servants to continue to speak your word with all boldness, while you stretch out your hand to heal, and signs and wonders are performed through the name of your holy servant Jesus." And when they had prayed, the place in which they were gathered together was shaken, and they were all filled with the Holy Spirit and continued to speak the word of God with boldness.

      The authority we were originally created to posses but which Adam handed over to the enemy in the fall has been restored! Jesus triumphed and took back all authority and gave it back to us. We have the authority to heal by the power of the Holy Spirit because of the blood of Christ Jesus!!

      Let's settle on this authority. All authority was originally given to us by God. To have dominion over our domain, the earth. We lost that authority and handed it over to satan at the fall. Jesus came and took all authority and gave it back to us. So all His authority is ours.

      Satan operates now under a false authority. The only authority he has is when sons/daughters don't utilize or walk in the authority we have been given in Christ Jesus.

Romans 8:19

The creation waits in eager expectation for the sons of God to be revealed.

It's like when a person is put in charge in some situation and given authority and then they simply don't lead and exercise their authority; someone else in the group will step up and take authority even though it wasn't given to them. This often leads to misusing or abusing authority. This will go on until the person given the authority starts to exercise it.

We have to utilize the authority given to us because the earth is our domain not the devils anymore. He will continue to operate in false authority until the Father's sons and daughters understand they have all authority and use it. Faith is the key that unlocks the reality that the earth is now our domain and we have full rights to exercise the authority of heaven on earth.

Matthew 28:18-20

And Jesus came and said to them, "All authority in heaven and on earth has been given to me. Go therefore and make disciples of all nations, baptizing them in the name of the Father and of the Son and of the Holy Spirit, teaching them to observe all that I have commanded you. And behold, I am with you always, to the end of the age."

John 14:12-14

"Truly, truly, I say to you, whoever believes in me will also do the works that I do; and greater works than these will he do, because I am going to the Father. Whatever you ask in my name, this I will do, that the Father may be glorified in the Son. If you ask me anything in my name, I will do it.

Let's recap a little bit.

John 10:10

The thief does not come except to steal, and to kill, and to destroy. I have come that they may have life, and that they may have it more abundantly.

Now let's look at the word abundantly . (Perrisos) Strongs #4053. Superabundance, excessive, overflowing, surplus, over and above, more than enough, profuse, extraordinary!

What kind of life does God desire to give us? What is the highest expression of life? What kind of life were we originally created with, but lost, and Jesus came to get it back for us? Eternal Life! The very life of God!

John 3:15

that whoever believes in Him should not perish but have eternal life.

John 6:54

Whoever eats My flesh and drinks My blood has eternal life, and I will raise him up at the last day.

What is eternal life?

John 17:3

And this is eternal life, that they may know You, the only true God, and Jesus Christ whom You have sent.

You could also say eternal life is the very life of God. It's His life dispensed into you. How does God want you to know Him? Abundantly

You could read John 10:10 like this....

The thief does not come except to steal, and to kill, and to destroy....

I have come that you may know me and be so excessively filled with my life that the over abundance of my life in you will overflow everywhere you go!

It's so important to get to know God. When you get to know Him you will understand what comes from God and what doesn't. Many people think that some of the worst tragedies in their life come from God. Remember, there is a real enemy out there operating under false authority, and his sole mission is to steal, kill, and destroy. And in the midst of it all, his secondary mission is to convince people that God is to blame for his doings.

Here are some phrases the enemy likes to hear. "God, why are you doing this to me.""God, why did you take my son." "I don't understand why God would allow this to happen." "God is allowing me to go through this to teach me something. "God is not out to destroy you!

He came to give you life and power to overcome the one trying to destroy you! In Him you are more than a conquerer! Each one of you is a son or daughter of the most High God! So let's be rock solid in our identity where nothing can shake us! We are unshakable! Let's get out there and love people, pray with authority, and put our hands on the sick! It's time to Become Love!

Chapter 8

BAPTISM OF THE HOLY SPIRIT

The Baptism of the Holy Spirit is a very misunderstood truth within the church today. When we don't have a revelation of something or an understanding, we tend to fear what we do not understand. When we don't understand something and a spirit of fear comes over it we tend to close ourselves off from it.

In this session we will hopefully clear up any confusion that may exist and get a clear understanding from the scriptures. Then we will cast out the spirit of fear and ask God to Baptize us in His Spirit.

Romans 10:17

So faith comes from hearing, and hearing through the word of Christ.

So let's take a look at the Word and let truth settle in our hearts so we can live by faith. Let's start in John 4 with the story of Jesus and the Woman of Samaria. Read this whole story if you are unfamiliar.

John 4:10

"If you knew the gift of God, and who it is that is saying to you, 'Give me a drink,' you would have asked him, and he would have given you living water."

Matthew 7:7

"Ask and it will be given to you; knock, and it will be opened to you. For everyone who asks receives, and the one who seeks finds, and to the one who knocks it will be opened."

John 4:13

"Everyone who drinks of this water will be thirsty again, but whoever drinks of the water that I will give him will never be thirsty again. The water that I will give him will become in him a spring of water welling up to eternal life."

Jesus is talking about thirst hear but what He is really getting at is spiritual fulfillment. This is Jesus telling you He is your fullness, He is your identity, He is the one that makes you complete. When you are thirsty in your soul and thirsty in your spirit it means you are not settled, satisfied, convinced or fulfilled.

Ephesians 3:19

and to know the love of Christ that surpasses knowledge, that you may be filled with all the fullness of God.

The word fullness means a house with no empty rooms, a town with no empty houses, a ship so full of cargo there is no space to put another box. That can be your life by understanding who you are in Him.

"a spring of water welling up to eternal life."

Here He is talking about being born again. Having your spirit recreated. He is talking about you receiving the life of Christ on the inside as a seal of the day of redemption.

John 7:37-39 *(Underlined my emphasis)*

On the last day of the feast, the great day, Jesus stood up and <u>cried out</u>, "If anyone thirsts, let him come to me and

drink. Whoever believes in me, <u>as the Scripture has said, Out of his heart will flow rivers of living water.'" Now this he said about the Spirit, whom those who believed in him were to receive, for as yet the Spirit had not been given, because Jesus was not yet glorified.</u>

This passage is similar to John 4; however in John 4 the language says "spring of water welling up to eternal life," talking about the born again experience. This passage is more intense; "out of his heart with flow rivers of living water." As you can see this is two different experiences. Keep reading and you will see this is referring to receiving the baptism of the Holy Spirit.

John 19-22 (Underlined my emphasis)

"Peace be with you. As the Father has sent me, even so I am sending you." And when he had said this, <u>he breathed on them and said to them, "Receive the Holy Spirit."</u>

What did they receive here when Jesus did this? In this moment they were born again. You could say their spirit was made holy. This was their born again experience. They have been redeemed. They were brought back to Genesis 1 when God breathed life into Adam. That breath was lost in the fall through sin and now Jesus restored that breath through His cross and resurrection, and Jesus Himself breathed life back into man. "Receive the Holy Spirit."

Now if you look at **Luke 24:49**

"And behold, I am sending the promise of my Father upon you. But stay in the city until you are clothed with power from on high."

In John 20 He breathed on them and said "receive Holy Spirit," but here He says stay put until you are "clothed with power."

Acts 1:4-5;8

And while staying with them he ordered them not to depart from Jerusalem, but to wait for the promise of the Father, which, he said, "you heard from me; for John baptized with water, but you will be baptized with the Holy Spirit not many days from now."you will receive power when the Holy Spirit has come upon you, and you will be my witnesses.

Wait a minute Jesus, you already breathed on us and said "receive Holy Spirit," and now you are telling me to wait because Holy Spirit is coming; you already said He came? No He didn't, He said receive a recreated spirit, be born again, be re-fathered, become a child of God.

Now there is something different coming. You better hang around because God has something else coming that you don't want to miss. You are going to be immersed into the Holy Spirit and He is going to empower you to be His witness and **"if you believe as the scriptures have said, out of your heart will flow rivers of living water." "This He spoke of the Spirit."**

Read **Acts 2** to see the fulfillment of what Jesus told them would happen.

Then in **Acts 8:14-17** (Underlined my emphasis)

Now when the apostles at Jerusalem heard that Samaria had received the word of God, they sent to them Peter and John, who came down <u>and prayed for them that they might receive the Holy Spirit, for he had not yet fallen on any of them, but they had only been baptized in the name of the Lord Jesus. Then they laid their hands on them and they received the Holy Spirit.</u>

Well now I thought you received the Holy Spirit when you are born again? It's true in the sense of a recreated spirit, "receive Holy Spirit." But then "you will receive power when the Holy Spirit comes upon you."

Luke 11:13

If you then, who are evil, know how to give good gifts to your children, how much more will the heavenly Father give the Holy Spirit to those who ask him!

Here's a question: Why do you ask for the Holy Spirit if He's automatic? As we can see above in Acts 8, Samaria heard the gospel from Phillip and got born again; however Peter and John were sent because they had only (not less significant) received water baptism, but Holy Spirit had not yet fallen on them. It looks like this was something pretty important for Peter and John to walk about 50 miles in that day to lay hands on them so that they may receive the Holy Spirit. If Holy Spirit is automatic with your salvation experience then why is this here?

Acts 8:17

Then they laid their hands on them and they received the Holy Spirit.

Acts 8:18-24

Now when Simon saw that the Spirit was given through the laying on of the apostles' hands, he offered them money, saying, "Give me this power also, so that anyone on whom I lay my hands may receive the Holy Spirit." But Peter said to him, "May your silver perish with you, because you thought you could obtain the gift of God with money! You have neither part nor lot in this matter, for your heart is not right before God. Repent, therefore, of this wickedness of yours, and pray to the Lord that, if possible, the intent of your heart may be forgiven you. For I see that you are in the gall of bitterness and in the bond of iniquity." And Simon answered,

"Pray for me to the Lord, that nothing of what you have said may come upon me."

If you look at this, Simon obviously saw some kind of physical manifestation after they had laid hands on them. The only real manifestation the Bible speaks about with the Baptism of the Holy Spirit is speaking in tongues. Again, the problem that comes up is the misrepresentation of speaking in tongues and people not understanding it, so they fear it and disregard it.

Speaking in tongues is a way of edifying yourself and communicating to the Holy Spirit in a way that our earthly words simply can't match. Tongues is speaking blessings to God that our minds cannot conjure up on our own. It bypasses the mind and you speak directly from your spirit to His Spirit.

1 Corinthians 14:1-2 (*Underlined my emphasis*)

Pursue love, and earnestly desire the spiritual gifts, especially that you may prophesy. <u>For one who speaks in a tongue speaks not to men but to God</u>; for no one understands him, but he utters mysteries in the Spirit.

It is God's will that you speak to Him and worship Him with your mind and with your spirit.

1 Corinthians 14:15

For if I pray in a tongue, my spirit prays but my mind is unfruitful. What am I to do? I will pray with my spirit, but I will pray with my mind also; I will sing praise with my spirit, but I will sing with my mind also.

I believe this verse teaches us to first engage Him in prayer through the spirit and then let Him fill your mind with the understanding. This gift, just like any other, will need to be nurtured, stewarded and grown in. I encourage you to engage the Lord with your divine language and commit to growing in this. It will greatly impact your intimacy with the Lord and release understanding in your life like you have never known. This gift is for <u>everyone</u> who asks and receives by faith the baptism of the Holy Spirit.

Acts 10:44-48

While Peter was still saying these things, the Holy Spirit fell on all who heard the word. And the believers from among the circumcised who had come with Peter were amazed, because the gift of the Holy Spirit was poured out even on the Gentiles. For they were hearing them speaking in tongues and extolling God. Then Peter declared, "Can anyone withhold water for baptizing these people, who have received the Holy Spirit just as we have?" And he commanded them to be baptized in the name of Jesus Christ. Then they asked him to remain for some days.

     Peter is amazed and thinking Wow! The same thing that happened to us Jews in Acts 2 just happened to these Gentiles! Can anything stop this gospel? Baptize them in the name of Jesus for they have been saved! So in Samaria they got saved, were water baptized and then baptized in the Holy Spirit. Here they got baptized in the Holy Spirit, saved, and then water baptized. It's the power of the gospel for those who receive and believe!

Acts 19:1-10

And it happened that while Apollos was at Corinth, Paul passed through the inland country and came to Ephesus. There he found some disciples. And he said to them, "Did you receive the Holy Spirit when you believed?" And they said, "No, we have not even heard that there is a Holy Spirit." And he said, "Into what then were you baptized?" They said, "Into John's baptism." And Paul said, "John baptized with the baptism of repentance, telling the people to believe in the one who was to come after him, that is, Jesus." On hearing

this, they were baptized in the name of the Lord Jesus. And when Paul had laid his hands on them, the Holy Spirit came on them, and they began speaking in tongues and prophesying. There were about twelve men in all.

And he entered the synagogue and for three months spoke boldly, reasoning and persuading them about the kingdom of God. But when some became stubborn and continued in unbelief, speaking evil of the Way before the congregation, he withdrew from them and took the disciples with him, reasoning daily in the hall of Tyrannus. This continued for two years, so that all the residents of Asia heard the word of the Lord, both Jews and Greeks.

We see upon Paul meeting these people the very first thing he asked them was "Did you receive the Holy Spirit when you believed." Maybe Paul should get some understanding because you get the Holy Spirit when you are born again. I'm obviously being sarcastic because what we really see is Paul's most important thought was to make sure these disciples were to be endued with power to be a witness. If the Holy Spirit is automatic, then why is Paul asking the question?

So we have seen several examples where the Holy Spirit came upon the laying on of hands and others when He just came. Don't miss out on this amazing gift the Lord wants to bestow upon you. It's free and all you have to do is ask your Father for it and receive it by faith through the motive of love.

Chapter 9

SPIRITUAL GIFTS

The purpose of being baptized in the Holy Spirit is to reach people through love and power just like we see Jesus did during His time on earth. To be His witnesses we need to walk in the love of God and the power of God.

Before you can operate in the power of God it is critical you operate in the love of God first! If you don't understand who you are as a child of God, and become love, then you will try and draw your identity by how you are being used by God.

If you are going through this book, please don't skip to the power of God until you have gone through the rest of this material and learned about the love of God. Beyond that, don't commit to pursuing these spiritual gifts until your heart is set on becoming love.

1 Corinthians 13:1-3

If I speak in the tongues of men and of angels, but have not love, I am a noisy gong or a clanging cymbal. And if I have prophetic powers, and understand all mysteries and all knowledge, and if I have all faith, so as to remove mountains, but have not love, I am nothing. If I give away all I have, and if I deliver up my body to be burned, but have not love, I gain nothing.

Remember we are being transformed into the image of Christ and Jesus said our mission is to be like Him. So Jesus is our pattern of life and the basis of how we should think. Simply put, Christianity is about Transformation! It's the whole point of our rebirth! Just like Jesus, we become about our Father's business. Walking in Power and Love!

John 5:19-20

So Jesus said to them, "Truly, truly, I say to you, the Son can do nothing of his own accord, but only what he sees the Father doing. For whatever the Father does, that the Son does likewise. For the Father loves the Son and shows him all that he himself is doing. And greater works than these will he show him, so that you may marvel.

John 14:12-14

"Truly, truly, I say to you, whoever believes in me will also do the works that I do; and greater works than these will he do, because I am going to the Father. Whatever you ask in my name, this I will do, that the Father may be glorified in the Son. If you ask me anything in my name, I will do it.

So just as Jesus was endued with Power by the Holy Spirit, so have we through the baptism of the Holy Spirit. Now we can do the things Jesus did.

Acts 10:38

God anointed Jesus of Nazareth with the Holy Spirit and with power. He went about doing good and healing all who were oppressed by the devil, for God was with him.

Acts 1:8

But you will receive power when the Holy Spirit has come upon you, and you will be my witnesses in Jerusalem and in all Judea and Samaria, and to the end of the earth."

Now that we understand the will of God and the love of God, let's pursue these spiritual gifts so that we can also walk in the power of God and begin to understand the gifts the Holy Spirit has blessed us with so we can keep filling the earth with the image of God and His glory.

It's time to…."Be Fruitful and Multiply.""Be Fishers of Men.""Go therefore, and make disciples of all nations."

1 Corinthians 14:1

Pursue love, and earnestly desire the spiritual gifts.

As we dive into these spiritual gifts, it's important to keep in mind this study is meant to give a foundational understanding of the gifts of the Spirit. It is not an all-inclusive breakdown of each gifting. The level of understanding you will gain will allow you to pray into these gifts and pursue them in the secret place with the Lord.

There is a lot of debate on the subject of spiritual gifts; so I'm going to attempt to break this down into the simplest terms according to the scriptures. In a broad sense, spiritual gifts are broken down into Two Main Categories.

A. Ministry Gifts.

B. Manifestation Gifts.

A. MINISTRY GIFTS

Ephesians 4:1-16

I therefore, a prisoner for the Lord, urge you to walk in a manner worthy of the calling to which you have been called, with all humility and gentleness, with patience, bearing with one another in love, eager to maintain the unity of the Spirit in the bond of peace. There is one body and one Spirit—just as you were called to the one hope that belongs to your call— one Lord, one faith, one baptism, one God and Father of all, who is over all and through all and in all. But grace was given to each one of us according to the measure of Christ's gift. Therefore it says,

"When he ascended on high he led a host of captives, and he gave gifts to men."

(In saying, "He ascended," what does it mean but that he had also descended into the lower regions, the earth? He who descended is the one who also ascended far above all the heavens, that he might fill all things.) <u>And he gave the apostles, the prophets, the evangelists, the shepherds and teachers</u>, to equip the saints for the work of ministry, for building up the body of Christ, until we all attain to the unity of the faith and of the knowledge of the Son of God, to

mature manhood, to the measure of the stature of the fullness of Christ, so that we may no longer be children, tossed to and fro by the waves and carried about by every wind of doctrine, by human cunning, by craftiness in deceitful schemes. Rather, speaking the truth in love, we are to grow up in every way into him who is the head, into Christ, from whom the whole body, joined and held together by every joint with which it is equipped, when each part is working properly, makes the body grow so that it builds itself up in love.

These gifts or offices are designed to carry out the <u>Plans of God</u> and are charged with <u>Equipping and Building up the Body of Christ</u> for ministry/service.

- Apostles (apostolos) delegate, ambassador of the gospel.
- Prophets (prophetes) forteller, inspired speaker, a poet; prophet.
- Evangelists (euaggelistes) preacher of the gospel.
- Pastors (poimen) shepard, pastor.
- Teachers (didaskalos) instructor, doctor, master, teacher.

Romans 12:3-8 *(Underlined my emphasis)*

For by the grace given to me I say to everyone among you not to think of himself more highly than he ought to think, but to think with sober judgment, each according to the measure of faith that God has assigned. For as in one body we have many members, and the members do not all have the same function, so we, though many, are one body in

Christ, and individually members one of another. Having gifts that differ according to the grace given to us, let us use them: <u>if prophecy, in proportion to our faith; if service, in our serving; the one who teaches, in his teaching; the one who exhorts, in his exhortation; the one who contributes, in generosity; the one who leads, with zeal; the one who does acts of mercy, with cheerfulness.</u>

- Prophecy (propheteia) prediction, prophesying.

- Service (diakonia) attendance, aid, serving, relief, ministering.

- Teaching (didasko) to learn and teach.

- Exhortation (paraklesis) imploration, solace, comfort, consolation.

- Giving (metadidomi) to give over, share, give, impart.

- Administration (proistemi) to stand before, preside, be over, rule, to lead.

- Mercy (eleeo) compassionate, divine grace.

These type of gifts are designed to <u>Allow the Body of Christ (the church/eklesia) to Function as a Single Unit.</u>

1 Peter 4:10-11

As each has received a gift, use it to serve one another, as good stewards of God's varied grace: whoever speaks, as one who speaks oracles of God; whoever serves, as one who serves by the strength that God supplies—in order that in everything God may be glorified through Jesus Christ. To him belong glory and dominion forever and ever. Amen.

B. MANIFESTATION GIFTS

1 Corinthians 12:4-11

Now there are varieties of gifts, but the same Spirit; and there are varieties of service, but the same Lord; and there are varieties of activities, but it is the same God who empowers them all in everyone. To each is given the <u>manifestation of the Spirit</u> for the common good. For to one is given through the Spirit the utterance of <u>wisdom, and to another the utterance of knowledge according to the same Spirit, to another faith by the same Spirit, to another gifts of healing by the one Spirit, to another the working of miracles, to another prophecy, to another the ability to distinguish between spirits, to another various kinds of tongues, to another the interpretation of tongues.</u> All these are empowered by one and the same Spirit, who apportions to each one individually as he wills.

The Gifts of the Manifestation of the Spirit are generally broken down into three categories.

1. The Revelatory Gifts.

    - Word of Wisdom

    - Word of Knowledge

    - Discerning of Spirits

2. The Power Gifts.

    - Gift of Healing

    - Working of Miracles

- Gift of Faith

3. The Utterance Gifts.

- Gift of Tongues

- Interpretation of Tongues

- Prophecy

Let's begin to break these down; however keeping at the forefront of our minds that these are gracious gifts given to us to reach people with the gospel, not a magic formula to flow in power for our own sense of acceptance by God.

Each one of these categories has three gifts, and the Holy Spirit can gift you to flow in and out of each category depending on the situation to love in front of you.

THE REVELATORY GIFTS

Word of Knowledge:

A word of knowledge is supernatural information about a person that typically no one would know about or at least not upon just meeting a person. This could be anything form identifying a sickness to knowing their name, birthdate, or some other important date in their lives.

Many times words of knowledge come as visions as if you are seeing a movie clip played in your mind or simply hearing phrases in your mind. Often it's easy to think this is your imagination; however the more time you spend in intimacy with the Lord the easier it is to discern what you are seeing or hearing is from the Holy Spirit.

Words of knowledge could also manifest in feeling physical needs in your own body, showing you that person needs healing and prayer for that need.

Jesus operated in words of knowledge all the time and one example is found in

John 1:45-51

Philip found Nathanael and said to him, "We have found him of whom Moses in the Law and also the prophets wrote, Jesus of Nazareth, the son of Joseph." Nathanael said to him, "Can anything good come out of Nazareth?" Philip said to him, "Come and see." Jesus saw Nathanael coming toward him and said of him, "Behold, an Israelite indeed, in whom there is no deceit!" Nathanael said to him, "How do you know me?" Jesus answered him, "Before Philip called you, when you were under the fig tree, I saw you." Nathanael answered him, "Rabbi, you are the Son of God! You are the King of Israel!" Jesus answered him, "Because I said to you, 'I saw you under the fig tree,' do you believe? You will see greater things than these." And he said to him, "Truly, truly, I say to you, you will see heaven opened, and the angels of God ascending and descending on the Son of Man."

Operating in this gifting shows the heart of the Father to His sons and daughters because it shows people that God sees them and cares for them.

<u>Word of Wisdom:</u>

Words of wisdom and words of knowledge often flow with each other. Words of wisdom are supernatural insights to guide a person's actions in the present and the future. Words of knowledge typically deal with the present and past.

Again, there are many examples from the life of Jesus.

Matthew 22:15-22

Then the Pharisees went and plotted how to entangle him in his words. And they sent their disciples to him, along with the Herodians, saying, "Teacher, we know that you are true and teach the way of God truthfully, and you do not care about anyone's opinion, for you are not swayed by appearances. Tell us, then, what you think. Is it lawful to pay taxes to Caesar, or not?" But Jesus, aware of their malice, said, "Why put me to the test, you hypocrites? Show me the coin for the tax." And they brought him a denarius. And Jesus said to them, "Whose likeness and inscription is this?" They said, "Caesar's." Then he said to them, "Therefore render to Caesar the things that are Caesar's, and to God the things that are God's." When they heard it, they marveled. And they left him and went away.

Discerning of Spirits:

Discerning of Spirits is not the same thing as the gift of discernment. Technically there is no gift of discernment but rather the spiritual gift of discerning of spirits. The gift of discerning of spirits is the supernatural ability to differentiate between what is of the flesh, what is demonic, what is angelic, and what is of the Holy Spirit. This gift often prepares us for prophetic intersession and highlights what we need to battle in prayer. In Acts 8:18-24 Peter shows us an example of discerning motives of the flesh.

Acts 8:18-24

Now when Simon saw that the Spirit was given through the laying on of the apostles' hands, he offered them money, saying, "Give me this power also, so that anyone on whom I lay my hands may receive the Holy Spirit." But Peter said to him, "May your silver perish with you, because you thought you could obtain the gift of God with money! You have neither part nor lot in this matter, for your heart is not right before God. Repent, therefore, of this wickedness of yours, and pray to the Lord that, if possible, the intent of your heart may be forgiven you. For I see that you are in the gall of bitterness and in the bond of iniquity." And Simon answered, "Pray for me to the Lord, that nothing of what you have said may come upon me."

In Acts 16:16-18 Paul shows us an example of discerning a demon.

Acts 16:16-18

As we were going to the place of prayer, we were met by a slave girl who had a spirit of divination and brought her owners much gain by fortune-telling. She followed Paul and us, crying out, "These men are servants of the Most High God, who proclaim to you the way of salvation." And this she kept doing for many days. Paul, having become greatly annoyed, turned and said to the spirit, "I command you in the name of Jesus Christ to come out of her." And it came out that very hour.

In Acts 10:30-35 Peter shows us an example of discerning what is from Holy Spirit.

Acts 10:30-35

And Cornelius said, "Four days ago, about this hour, I was praying in my house at the ninth hour, and behold, a man stood before me in bright clothing and said, 'Cornelius, your prayer has been heard and your alms have been remembered before God. Send therefore to Joppa and ask for Simon who is called Peter. He is lodging in the house of Simon, a tanner, by the sea.' So I sent for you at once, and you have been kind enough to come. Now therefore we are all here in the presence of God to hear all that you have been commanded by the Lord." So Peter opened his mouth and said: "Truly I understand that God shows no partiality, but in every nation anyone who fears him and does what is right is acceptable to him.

Sometimes this gift is accompanied by smells. Demonic influences can sometimes be detected by a foul stench to the person with this gifting. This foul stench will usually manifest as a sulphur-like smell or something similar to rotting flesh or eggs.

On the other hand, the presence of the Holy Spirit can manifest a sweet warm smell. Many people with this gift can also fall into trances where they have visions of angles or demons in activity.

THE POWER GIFTS

Gifts of Healing:

We have already settled it in our min; it is the will of God to heal and every believer can lay their hands on the sick. The person who operates in the gift of healings typically has a specific gift for a certain kind of sickness or disease such as cancer, diabetes, arthritis, mental disorders, infertility, ect.

Sometimes while you are talking to someone and discussing a particular issue, someone with the gift of healings will feel a grace come over them from the Holy Spirit; a change in the environment will shift in the room, and then the person with this gift will pray for that specific healing.

Working of Miracles:

As we just learned it is God's will to heal; however healing is often progressive while the gift of miracles is seeing instant change in a person's situation. The dictionary defines a miracle as "an effect or extraordinary event in the physical world that surpasses all known human or natural powers and is ascribed to a supernatural cause."

The Greek word for miracle is dunamis. This speaks to the divine power of God to heal in supernatural ways. There are many examples of Jesus and His followers doing this in the scriptures. One example we see in Acts 19:11-12 is that Paul was operating in the gift of miracles so much that even handkerchiefs and aprons that he had touched were taken to the sick and their diseases left them and evil spirits came out.

<u>Gift of Faith:</u>

Operating in the gift of faith is living absolutely fearless; knowing that you can step out into what God has called you to do. The miraculous follows this kind of faith and is truly a gift given by God. It is different than growing in faith because this kind of faith is unmerited in nature. It truly is a gift given by God. Again, Paul gifts us an example of this kind of supernatural faith to proclaim the impossible.

Acts 27:20-26

When neither sun nor stars appeared for many days, and no small tempest lay on us, all hope of our being saved was at last abandoned. Since they had been without food for a long time, Paul stood up among them and said, "Men, you should have listened to me and not have set sail from Crete and incurred this injury and loss. Yet now I urge you to take heart, for there will be no loss of life among you, but only of the ship. For this very night there stood before me an angel of the God to whom I belong and whom I worship, and he said, 'Do not be afraid, Paul; you must stand before Caesar. And behold, God has granted you all those who sail with you.' So take heart, men, for I have faith in God that it will be exactly as I have been told. But we must run aground on some island."

Here is another example of Peter flowing in this gift.

Acts 3:1-16

Now Peter and John were going up to the temple at the hour of prayer, the ninth hour. And a man lame from birth was

being carried, whom they laid daily at the gate of the temple that is called the Beautiful Gate to ask alms of those entering the temple. Seeing Peter and John about to go into the temple, he asked to receive alms. And Peter directed his gaze at him, as did John, and said, "Look at us." And he fixed his attention on them, expecting to receive something from them. But Peter said, "I have no silver and gold, but what I do have I give to you. In the name of Jesus Christ of Nazareth, rise up and walk!" And he took him by the right hand and raised him up, and immediately his feet and ankles were made strong. And leaping up, he stood and began to walk, and entered the temple with them, walking and leaping and praising God. And all the people saw him walking and praising God, and recognized him as the one who sat at the Beautiful Gate of the temple, asking for alms. And they were filled with wonder and amazement at what had happened to him.

THE UTTERANCE GIFTS

<u>The Gift of Tongues:</u>

The gift of tongues is different than your personal prayer language that we spoke about during the baptism of the Holy Spirit. This gift often manifests when you are around different culture groups and people start to hear your prayer and worship in another language. At times you may flow in a language you do not understand so you can give the Father's heart to someone who speaks that language. Typically you will not understand what you are saying but will notice a shift in the sound from your regular prayer language to this type of language.

Interpretation of Tongues:

The interpretation of tongues is not the translation of tongues. This gift will typically interpret the meaning of what was spoken as opposed to actually understanding the dialect itself. Someone may give a lengthy message in tongues and only a short interpretation or vice versa. It's important to note that the same person may be the one speaking in tongues and interpreting or someone with this gift may interpret someone else's tongues message.

The Gift of Prophecy:

The gift of prophecy is different than than being able to prophesy which 1 Corinthians 14:1-5 tells us all to pursue with all our hearts more than any other gift.

1 Corinthians 14:1-5

Pursue love, and earnestly desire the spiritual gifts, especially that you may prophesy. For one who speaks in a tongue speaks not to men but to God; for no one understands him, but he utters mysteries in the Spirit. On the other hand, the one who prophesies speaks to people for their upbuilding and encouragement and consolation. The one who speaks in a tongue builds up himself, but the one who prophesies builds up the church. Now I want you all to speak in tongues, but even more to prophesy. The one who prophesies is greater than the one who speaks in tongues, unless someone interprets, so that the church may be built up.

This level of basic prophesying is for edifying, encouraging, consoling, and building up the church and does not make one a prophet. It's part of becoming and walking in love!

The gift of prophecy is a manifestation of the Sprit which gives supernatural foretelling, foresight, insight, or oversight.

Foresight: The ability to see into the future. To get a visual of what is to come.

Insight: The ability to see how something works or comes together.

Oversight: The ability to see how things work together, come together and place people together.

This gift can often be accompanied with a word of knowledge. When given a word of knowledge for someone it may be followed by how that person can fix or overcome what is going on in there life by receiving a word of prophecy.

Just like any other spiritual gift, the gift of prophecy takes time to steward and grow. It takes time to learn how to be sensitive to the timing in which God wants you to release a word of prophecy. This only happens when you continue to pursue intimacy with the Lord and His word.

As I said in the beginning of this chapter it is vital that you do no pursue operating in spiritual gifts until you understand the love of God. Remember you cannot know God apart from understanding the love of God.

1 John 4:7-8

Beloved, let us love one another, for love is from God, and whoever loves has been born of God and knows God. Anyone who does not love does not know God, because God is love.

This is so critical that Jesus gives us this very sober warning in Matthew 7 so we are not fooled into believing we know God just because we may operate in a spiritual gifting.

Matthew 7:21-23

Not everyone who says to me, 'Lord, Lord,' will enter the kingdom of heaven, but the one who does the will of my Father who is in heaven. On that day many will say to me, 'Lord, Lord, did we not prophesy in your name, and cast out demons in your name, and do many mighty works in your name?' And then will I declare to them, 'I never knew you; depart from me, you workers of lawlessness.'

Remember, as 1 Timothy teaches us, the whole goal of everything in this study is to become love.

1 Timothy 1:4-5

The aim of our charge is love that issues from a pure heart and a good conscience and a sincere faith.

2 Peter 1:12-14

Therefore I intend always to remind you of these qualities, though you know them and are established in the truth that you have. I think it right, as long as I am in this body, to stir you up by way of reminder.

1 Corinthians 14:1

Pursue love, and earnestly desire the spiritual gifts.

CONCLUSION

In all your getting, get understanding

My hope and prayer is that you have a better understanding of the Gospel of the Kingdom and have embraced your true identity as a son or daughter within the Kingdom.

I hope you see how much value and significance your life has! Don't ever for a moment let the enemy convince you otherwise!

Remember, Jesus did not shed His blood because you were a sinner but rather a lost son/daughter and He is the way back to the Father.

You are a Son/Daughter.

You are The Body of Christ.

You are the Bride of Christ.

You were Made for the Kingdom.

You were Made for His Image!

Matthew 28:19-20

Go therefore and make disciples of all nations, baptizing them in the name of the Father and of the Son and of the

Holy Spirit, teaching them to observe all that I have commanded you. And behold, I am with you always, to the end of the age."

Genesis 1:28

And God blessed them. And God said to them, "Be fruitful and multiply.

Habakkuk 2:14

For the earth will be filled with the knowledge of the glory of the Lord.

Isaiah 6:3

And one called to another and said: "Holy, holy, holy is the Lord of hosts; the whole earth is full of his glory!"

www.ingramcontent.com/pod-product-compliance
Lightning Source LLC
Chambersburg PA
LVHW060948050426
737CB00052B/1971